CHILD SPIRIT

CHILD SPIRIT

Children's Experience with God in School

SAMUEL SILVERSTEIN

Introduced by David Spangler

BEAR & COMPANY
PUBLISHING

SANTA FE, NEW MEXICO

LIBRARY OF CONGRESS CATALOGING-IN-PUBLICATION DATA
Silverstein, Samuel.
   Child spirit: children's experience with God in school / by
Samuel Silverstein; foreword by David Spangler.
      p.   cm.
   Includes bibliographical references.
   ISBN 0-939680-81-5 (pbk.)
   1. Children—Religious life—Case studies. 2. Children—
Psychic Ability—Case studies. I. Title.
BL625.5.S55 1991
291.4'2'083—dc20   91-40222
                                                           CIP

Bear & Company, Inc.
Santa Fe, NM 87504-2860

Cover illustration: Kathleen Katz
Cover & interior design: Angela Werneke
Interior renditions of the children's drawings: Kathleen Katz
Author photo: Bill Bastenbeck, *The Register-Citizen*
Editing: Gail Vivino
Typography: Buffalo Publications
Printed in the United States of America by R.R. Donnelley

1 3 5 7 9 8 6 4 2

In truth I tell you,
unless you change and become like little children,
you will never enter the kingdom of heaven.

— Matthew 18:3

To all young children, wherever they might be,
who may have a "new world" within them.

CONTENTS

Illustrations xiii
Acknowledgments xv
Foreword by David Spangler xvii
Introduction 3

PART I: THE CHILDREN'S EXPERIENCES

The First Clue 7
In Search of a Method 10
The Notebooks 13
The Children's Reactions 14
Gail Hits Her Head on the Ceiling 16
More Out-of-Body Experiences 19
An Eight-Year-Old Sees God 20
In Search of the Truth 24
Attuning the Human Body 25
What Are the Vibrations? 26
The Intelligence within the Vibrations 28
A Theory of Life 33
Piaget and the Child 36
The Old Man Who Wasn't There 37
A Departed Grandmother Returns 42
Cosmic Consciousness 46
A New Science 49
A Particle of Light 51
How Light Was Seen to Travel 52
Electricity and Magnetism 53
Another Idea about the Atom 55
The Quantum Theory and Plant Growth 56

PART II: PSYCHIC CHILDREN AND THE BIBLE— IS THERE A CONNECTION?

Psychic Children and the Bible—Is There a Connection?...... 61

The Hand of the Lord Was Strong upon Me 62

The Heavens Were Opened 64

Living Creatures Appeared in a Flash of Lightning.......... 66

Moses and the Burning Bush 68

For God Is Love 71

That Christ May Dwell in Your Hearts 76

A Voice Came out of the Cloud 78

The Kingdom of God Is within Us 82

The Star of Bethlehem................................ 85

My Heart Is Glad.................................... 87

Jesus Casts out Unclean Spirits........................ 88

Seeing Angels...................................... 94

God in Heaven 98

PART III: CLASSROOM DISCUSSIONS

Brainstorming in the Classroom 103

Feeling the Vibrations 104

Feeling Peace within the Body 107

Falling Asleep...................................... 110

Feeling the Power of God 112

Electricity in the Body............................... 116

Peacefulness and the "Little Men" 118

Music from Heaven.................................. 121

The Third Eye 122

Psychic Children and the Near-Death Experience 124

PART IV: PRAYERS IN SCHOOL

A Moment of Silent Meditation 131
A Program for School Prayers 134
Keeping Religion out of the Classroom 135
Free the Children! 136

PART V: THE AUTHOR'S EXPERIENCES

Thoughts on my Background 141
The Experience in the Chapel 141
The Experience in the Mountains 145

Conclusion 155
Bibliography 157
About the Author 161

ILLUSTRATIONS

FIGURES

Figure 1. How Jesus Was Seen on Earth 31

Figure 2. The Sun and Moon Theory of Life 38

Figure 3. Cosmic Consciousness 47

Figure 4. The Spiral of a Light Particle 52

Figure 5. A Line of Light 52

Figure 6. Spinning Balls of Light 53

Figure 7. Electromagnetic Current 54

Figure 8. Quantum Growth in an Oat Stalk 56

Figure 9. "The Hand of the Lord Was Strong upon Me." 63

Figure 10. "Living Creatures Appeared in a Flash
of Lightning." 67

Figure 11. "For God Is Love." 74

Figure 12. "That Christ May Dwell in Your Hearts." 77

Figure 13. "A Voice Came out of the Cloud." 80

Figure 14. A Voice Calling in the Night 81

Figure 15. Good and Bad Spirits Inside the Body 91

Figure 16. An Angel Defeats an Evil Spirit 92

Figure 17. The Good Spirit 93

Figure 18. The Angel's Halo 97

Figure 19. Falling Asleep 111

Figure 20. Electricity in the Body 117

Figure 21. The Tunnel—A Gateway to Heaven 126

Figure 22. Rising Toward Heaven 127

PLATES

Plate 1. An Out-of-Body Experience

Plate 2. The Healing Hand

Plate 3. A Friend Materialized

Plate 4. "The Heavens Were Opened."

Plate 5. Moses and the Burning Bush

Plate 6. "My Heart Is Glad."

Plate 7. The Bad Spirit

Plate 8. Music from Heaven

ACKNOWLEDGMENTS

I would first like to thank the eight-year-old children in my third-grade classes, who had the courage, even sometimes only in whispers, to tell me of their inner experiences, which no one else seemed to take the time to understand. I have changed their names here to respect and protect their privacy.

Thanks also to Maria Montessori for discovering a "new world" within children. She made her discovery in 1906 with preschool children. Without previous knowledge of her work, I also made a similar discovery with older children in a public school classroom.

Finally, my thanks to the editors at Bear & Company, who showed the first interest in what I had researched and written about after many years of struggling.

FOREWORD

In Celtic lore, worlds of wonder, magic, and spirit are always near at hand, often as close as the other side of the nearest hedge. A mere step past a seemingly innocent and ordinary-looking tree or stone or bush, and suddenly you are in the Other World, a place of spiritual power, in the company of angels or other beings of light.

Most traditional and native cultures enjoy a sense of the closeness of the spiritual world. They know through both story and experience how that world continually and intimately interacts with our own. In our culture, though, we have largely lost that knowledge. For us, the spiritual world is usually seen as distant and separate, assuming we believe in it at all.

However, that attitude is changing. On the one hand, modern science is unveiling for us a vision of a universe woven of fields and patterns of energy, a universe in which everything that exists is connected in its deepest essence with everything else, while at the same time increasing numbers of people are having their own personal encounters with a larger reality through psychic and mystical experiences. In either case, we are again encountering the reality of the invisible and relearning what earlier cultures took for granted: that it is what we don't perceive with our physical senses that may be the most real and may have the most effect upon us.

Opening the portals of perception to reengage in co-creative ways with the reality of the spiritual world is as much a matter of attitude as it is of technique. As adults, most of us have been trained into an attitude that says such portals either don't exist, or, if they do, they should be kept closed. This is like saying that we should never raise the blinds or open the shutters in our houses lest we see a larger world outside. We should be content with just what is inside the house and not venture to play outside in the sunlight of a larger environment.

Fortunately, children seek the outdoors and the sunlight. They have an affinity for that larger world because they have not yet been conditioned otherwise. The attitudes of disbelief, fear, or confinement have not yet been developed—everything and anything is possible. It is not surprising, then, that through the consciousness of a child we can gain a glimpse of a greater dimension to our world, a dimension that we, as adults, may once have known and can know again.

This book is about the portal afforded us by the consciousness of children to see into the wider realms of spirit. It is not that children necessarily see the truth of that larger world and we do not, but that they are open to a broader vista of reality and hence open to aspects of truth that as adults we may be ignoring or have forgotten.

There is a regrettable tendency among adults to dismiss the perceptions of children as make-believe (as if much of what we think and do as adults is not also a form of make-believe, though more sophisticated). Yet, as a parent of three small children myself, I have often found their insights to be wise and accurate. Children may lack a language to give form to their experiences, but that doesn't mean the experiences are invalid.

My own spiritual perceptions and work began when I was a child. At the age of seven, I had a profound mystical experience of traveling out of my body and entering a condition of absolute unity with all of the world. It was not an isolated incident in my life, and I was fortunate to have parents and adult friends who honored these experiences and helped me explore their meaning. However, it was years before I developed a language and a conceptual skill to translate my inner experiences into words and images for others.

One problem with all spiritual perception is our tendency to take images literally. Children do this automatically; the knowledge that something may be symbolic or representative of something else develops with maturity—it is not inborn. Children do not distinguish the symbolic from the real. Misplaced concreteness can result. On the other hand, children do have an innocence that often allows them, or so it has been my experience, to see through the image to its essence. They may accept the symbol as real, but they go beyond it at the same time to the heart of what it represents. A child who sees a shining figure may see that being as Jesus, since Jesus (or God) is often the only image of spiritual power and presence that the child knows. However, whether it is Jesus or not, what the child really responds to is the essential presence of love and wholeness that this figure embodies and brings.

An adult having a psychic experience may also be unable to distinguish at first between an image that is symbolic and one that is "real," though at a nonphysical level of existence. Unlike a child, however, the adult may become overly attached to the symbol and the image and fail to go deeper to consider the actual essential nature of what he or she is contacting. For example, it has been my experience that the most trivial and even nonsensical material received by psychic means can be accepted uncritically if it is felt the source is Jesus, Buddha, or some other image of spiritual authority and greatness. Misplaced concreteness is as much, if not more, of a problem for adults than it is for children, particularly as we allow our egos to become attached to and invested in the "rightness" of our perceptions in ways that children generally do not.

Children may be natural mystics and have a wisdom born of their innocence, but they also usually lack experience, which can translate into an inability to discern fully what they are experiencing, though they can tell pretty well whether it is beneficial or not. Here is where a sympathetic and honoring adult consciousness can be very important. The child's inner discernment and insight can develop naturally if they are not quashed by ridicule, fear, or disbelief.

There is a resource in children that should be neither romanticized or inflated nor ignored or disbelieved. The perception of children of the wonderment and fullness of our world is generally less conditioned and more open than that of most adults. Taken in perspective, the insights and experiences of children with spiritual dimensions can help us restore our own sense of connection and closeness with those realms. They can teach us the vision inherent in wonder and innocence, to which we can add the vision rich in wisdom and experience.

That is the delight of this book. The author became childlike himself, and we can feel his wonder as he explored the potentialities and experiences of his pupils through very simple exercises. At the same time, he brought to the enterprise his experience and insights as an adult who could use the children's perceptions as steps into a more mature investigation. The author speculates, and you may or may not agree with all his conclusions and speculations, but he does so while retaining the sense of wonder and delight at the closeness of the spiritual reality. Further, one can sense innocence in him, for his speculations never become dogma but only invitations to our own discernment and exploration.

Like in Celtic lore, the author's classroom became his hedge and his children his guides into the Other World. Or we might say that his pupils were an indigenous, native people, their perceptions still close to the primal energies of nature and God, and he the anthropologist who came to live among them for a time.

In either case, Mr. Silverstein stepped into a new world and entered the tribe of childhood with grace and a deep spiritual sensitivity of his own, recorded what he found and now offers that record to us to enhance our own explorations of spirit. At a time when many adult voices are increasingly being raised to testify to the reality, power, and presence of the spiritual worlds, the author reminds us of a voice close at home, the voice of our children— and, just as importantly, of the child within us—that also speaks with experience of a spiritual domain as close to us as the suppleness of our imaginations and the openness of our hearts.

David Spangler
Issaquah, Washington
September 1991

David Spangler was formerly codirector of the Findhorn Foundation; *he is coauthor of* Reimagination of the World *and author of* Revelation: Birth of a New Age.

CHILD SPIRIT

INTRODUCTION

Tucked away in my attic for many years were some notebooks that I had placed there a long time ago. In those notebooks were things I had written down while I was a teacher to young children in a public school—things that so amazed me that I was afraid to tell very many people about them.

In those notebooks were experiences of a religious nature that as far as I knew might never have been described before, experiences that had happened to children that far surpassed anything that might have happened to their parents. In the classroom, however, the subject of religion was never mentioned.

This information came from ordinary eight-year-old children in a public school. It contained the kind of things an adult might hear from a child, attribute to the child's imagination, and let it go at that.

However, having been educated in the field of science and trained to search for facts and follow any lead wherever it might take me, I found another story. It is a story that tells how young children may experience the forces of God going through their bodies, perhaps every day. This phenomenon is not based on a religious upbringing, but simply on an inborn ability that, I feel, all children have. This is a realm still to be explored in depth by child psychologists.

The information in the notebooks left me in a state of awed bewilderment, and I kept quiet for a long time. But as I am getting along in years, I have come to the point where I must speak out and let the public decide about the validity of the information described in this book. I feel sure that now there will be a greater receptivity to these experiences than there would have been when they occurred almost forty years ago.

I believe that all young children live in two worlds, both at the same time, interlocked with each other: the ordinary world that we all see as children move about in daily life, and a "hidden world" in which they are in contact with God's presence. In 1906, Maria Montessori, the founder of the famous schools that bear her name, announced the existence of what she called a "new world" within children, and within two years that idea had spread globally. I would, however, call her "new world" rather a "hidden world," which is available to children all the time in early childhood, but after about the age of eight or so starts disappearing. Eventually, it becomes mostly a "lost world" — the lost world of childhood. As adults, unless we have the ability to recall those experiences of childhood, we will have at best only hazy memories of what once occurred.

In Gallup polls taken of adults in the United States, it has been found that most people "believe there is a God," though they have never seen God. Where might this belief come from? Perhaps it is the result of a faint recollection of God from their childhood!

I was able to do three years of research work with third-grade students. My findings indicate the possibility that children are more highly attuned than adults as far as having and describing religious experiences are concerned. (This is true regarding psychic experiences as well, as the two are closely related.)

The pages that follow contain the experiences of the children as I recorded them in my notebooks . . . now so long ago.

PART I
The Children's Experiences

THE FIRST CLUE

As it was written in the Dead Sea Scrolls, the Hebrew mystics of the past believed that if people on Earth could achieve harmony within themselves and become properly attuned, they could talk with God. These and other mystics of the past believed that the secret to the human body's becoming attuned to God lay in solving the riddles of the vibrations that exist throughout the universe, vibrations that also exist within the human body.

It was during my first month of teaching in the third grade of a public school in a small New England city in 1952 that I got the first clue about such vibrations. Maureen was the girl who gave it to me. She was the first one to stand up in class and say that she could look inside her body and see a vibration.

This happened after a morning recess period. The children had been playing quite hard out in the playground, and after coming back into the classroom, some were still breathing quite heavily and perspiring. I therefore allowed them to put their heads down on their desks to cool off and relax before starting their regular classwork.

To help the children relax, I had given them a yoga-type breathing exercise to do when they had their heads down. They would breathe in deeply, hold the air in their lungs for four or five seconds, and then slowly let the air drain out. As they exhaled slowly, the children would imagine that all the tiredness in their bodies was draining away with the outgoing breath. When the air was all out, they would sit quietly and wait several seconds before they

7

would repeat the process. After three or four such deep breaths and a few minutes of silent rest, the class would be ready to go back to work.

During such a quiet rest period, Maureen suddenly started to giggle. In the quiet room, her giggle was heard all over. Later on, when the rest period was over and all the heads were up, I asked her why she had laughed.

"I saw a worm wiggling down my arm," Maureen said in a loud voice. The class laughed when they heard this. I had to laugh myself. Children have a good imagination, and perhaps this was an example of it, but most children don't talk about having a worm wiggle down their arms.

My curiosity was aroused. Why should this girl imagine a worm wiggling down her arm? While the rest of the class was working, I called Maureen up to my desk and quietly questioned her some more.

"Yes," she said, "I saw what looked like a worm wiggling down the inside of my arm."

"What do you mean, 'looked like a worm'?"

"Well," Maureen said, "it wasn't a worm, but it wiggled like one, and I didn't know what else to call it."

"You said you saw it inside your arm. Do you really mean you could see inside your arm?"

"That's right," she said. "I saw it moving inside my arm. It was sort of a yellow color, and when it wiggled toward the outside where my skin was, that made it tickle. So I laughed."

Maureen's story left me a little shaken up. The girl had told it in such a convincing manner—as if it had actually happened.

For the rest of the day I tried to forget what Maureen had told me, but it kept creeping back into my mind. At the end of the day, after all the children had gone, my thoughts went back again to the "wiggling worm." At that point a thought hit me that left me somewhat dazed: the story the girl had told me might be true! This realization came to me as I sat there in the solitude of the empty room. Then I suddenly remembered from my own past an experience that I had had. It was very similar to the girl's story.

The whole incident swiftly came back to me, and I reexperienced it almost as vividly as when it had occurred almost ten years before. During World War II, in Italy, I was a lieutenant with the infantry. There was a lull in the fighting at one point, and I had time to shave a heavy growth of whiskers off my face. In the process of shaving, I was suddenly surprised to see a wiggly line appear inside my left cheek. It was about an inch long and yellowish in color. It seemed to me that I saw it not with my ordinary eyes, but in some other manner, as if I were out in front of myself and able to see inside my body.

Both the girl and I saw a wiggly line. It was yellow in color to both of us. And we both saw it—in some mysterious manner— inside our bodies. It seemed that my wiggly line, or perhaps it would be more accurate to call it a vibration, had already wiggled by the time I saw it. The wiggles had been rigid in their formation. However, the wiggly line in the girl's arm was moving, and this made her giggle. The wiggly line in my cheek had not done that, but instead it had filled my body with such an awesome feeling of blissfulness that when a sudden barrage of enemy artillery scattered nearby soldiers, I just continued sitting there, enjoying this strange, peaceful, inner feeling.

My sudden realization that what Maureen had described to me could have been a true experience made me wonder. What was the meaning of such a wiggly line inside the human body? If one child could see it, were other children able to experience the same thing?

After questioning the class several days later, I discovered indications that other children also felt things, and even saw things, inside their bodies. Even though I had experienced such a flash of "inner vision" in only one rare moment of my life, the children in the classroom gave indications that this happened to them frequently.

What went on inside these children? I didn't know. Perhaps, in the classroom, there would be a chance to find out. Perhaps some research could be done to find out more about the vibrations. Perhaps a clearer understanding of children would come to me so that I could do a better job as their teacher.

IN SEARCH OF A METHOD

How can one go looking for vibrations in a public school classroom—vibrations that the mystics said might lead people to God? I tried it. As a beginning teacher who didn't know any better, I tried looking for God in the public school classroom.

In our school, at that point in time, a teacher could still have the children bow their heads in the morning during the opening exercises and repeat the Lord's Prayer aloud. However, it was forbidden for the teacher to discuss anything about prayer with the children at all. That was the school system's policy, and I respected that regulation.

There was, however, one time period during the day that could be used for questioning children about prayer, and it was already part of the approved school curriculum. This one spot was the last half hour of school on Friday. An art period had been scheduled for that time, or, as an old planbook called it, a "creative expression" period, a term I liked very much. I learned when I first began teaching that this half hour had been used in the past by an art teacher to work with the children. However, no art teacher had been hired for the first year that I was teaching. Instead, the school principal had given the regular classroom teacher permission to use this period to work with the class in any form of creative expression that he or she wished.

Therefore, I had found a period of time to carry out the ideas that were creeping into my mind, but how was I to go about finding a method to implement these ideas? What was a way to discover what actually goes on inside a child's "inner world"?

Perhaps the old mystics of the past—the mystics of the Far East—could give me a clue to a method. They had described things going on in the invisible world that they claimed they could see. To do this, they went into caves to meditate, to be alone, to pray, and to attune their bodies so that they could experience the unknown within themselves.

This might have been similar to the relaxation method I had been using in the classroom. This method involved having the kids put their heads down on their desks, relax their bodies, and also do some deep breathing as they sat there quietly. It was while doing this relaxation exercise that Maureen suddenly had seen a vibration moving inside her arm.

Based on these thoughts, I developed a method that had some similarities to the ways of the mystics. For solitude, the kids would put their heads down on their desks and close their eyes, which would shut out their surroundings. For complete silence, there would be no talking at any time while their heads were down. The kids would do the deep breathing exercise several times to help them relax and attune their bodies so that things could happen. For meditation, I would have them concentrate on one idea at a time—an idea that the kids first expressed themselves and one that I usually didn't know anything about myself.

An example of where I got these ideas was Maureen's experience of seeing the wiggly line in her body. Based on this experience, I asked the kids questions, but I asked only one question during each Friday afternoon period. Some of the questions were the following: If you can see wiggly lines, as Maureen did, what different colors do they have? Do they always wiggle, or do they move in other ways? Where do the wiggly lines come from?

Before I had the kids do the relaxation exercise, we would have a lively discussion about the idea of the day. I would listen to the different things the children had to say, but I wouldn't pay too much attention to these initial comments because this part of the technique simply acted as a way to speed up their minds to a higher level of interest.

After several minutes of these quick comments from the children, I would suddenly cut off all discussion and then have them do the following, which usually produced good results:

> The kids would put their heads down on their desks, close their eyes, and relax their bodies by taking deep breaths. Within a short time they would start concentrating on the idea chosen for that day. When they saw pictures in their minds that they thought could be shown in a drawing (this took about ten seconds), they would lift up their heads and start to draw. Paper had been passed out previously and was on their desks.
>
> The children were quiet at all times and did not show their drawings to anyone else. If there was time, they would also

write about their experiences as best they could. While they were drawing and writing, I would move about the classroom, glancing quickly here and there at their drawings. If a drawing had lots of action in it, I would ask questions quietly, or even make a few notes or place arrows on it to show more clearly what the drawing was about, so I wouldn't forget later on.

After most of the drawings were completed, I would ask for volunteers to come up to the front of the room. With their drawings in their hands, these children would then tell the others what they had experienced.

There were only thirty minutes to this creative-expression period, so a fast pace had to be maintained if most of the children were to finish drawing the things they were able to see in their inner worlds. At the end of the period the drawings were collected. If any children wanted to keep their drawings, they could do so. I saved the rest of the drawings. I took them home, examined them more carefully, and recorded the main points of information about them in notebooks while they were still fresh in my mind.

The art paper used for most of the drawings was plain yellow paper that had been cut in half. This size was small enough for the children to finish drawing within the half-hour allotted time, yet large enough to allow for detail.

Some of the children, however, when they tried to show what happened inside of them, took too much time drawing the shape of their bodies. By the time they were ready to draw what happened inside their bodies, there was not enough time left in the period. So if any children raised their hands, I would go over to them and draw a gingerbread-person figure for them with one motion of my pencil. The children could then go on to draw what actually happened inside their bodies, which was the important part.

The children used ordinary school crayons that were passed out to them at the beginning of the school year. They were told to be as accurate as they could and to use the same colors in their drawings as they saw in their own experiences, if possible.

This, in general, was the method I used to gather information on the experiences that the children had. I filled up many notebooks on the inner world that these children were able to see.

THE NOTEBOOKS

For the first three years of my teaching, until an art teacher was hired for the school (at which point my research stopped), I continued to work with the eight-year-old children during the creative expression period.

During this entire period, I recorded in notebooks the things the children talked about while this information was still fresh in my mind, sometimes working until one or two o'clock in the morning. In addition, several thousand of the children's drawings were saved and stored away because I hoped someday to understand them better.

These kids described a world that was visible to them but invisible to me. Many of the things they could see and feel were described over and over again, as if there might have been a basic science to their invisible world about which modern adults know very little.

The children talked of colored vibrations coming down from the sky to pass through their bodies along regular pathways. They saw electricity coming from their fingertips. They experienced tiny explosions inside their bodies that caused them to fall asleep. They saw and heard voices moving along vibrations inside their bodies.

By the time an art teacher was finally hired, I had just about stopped gathering material anyway, because I was stymied. I didn't know where to go next. I didn't know what to do with the notebooks or the drawings.

I had written many letters to leading authorities in the country who might have known more about the inner world of children. There was no help there. Dr. Arnold Gesell, who was still alive and at his Institute of Child Development at Yale University, wrote back and said he couldn't help me. Dr. Joseph Rhine, at Duke University, was conducting his card experiments in ESP at that time and wanted me to do the same thing with my class. I didn't want to do this. After sending a letter to Dr. Karl Menninger at the Menninger Foundation, I received an answer saying that my children were just having the fantasies that all children have. I felt that this answer was wrong.

After six years of teaching the third grade, the principal of the school asked me to move up to the seventh-grade level to teach science. I found that the abilities of the third-grade children had already been lost by the time these same children reached the seventh grade. In the lower grade, after several months of doing the relaxation exercise, between twenty and twenty-five children out of a class of about thirty could turn in drawings regularly that depicted the inner world they could see. In the higher grade, perhaps one or two of the children could do such a drawing, and then one only of minor significance.

William Wordsworth wrote of this phenomenon in his famous "Ode: Intimations of Immortality from Recollections of Early Childhood." He calls the young child a "mighty prophet," but laments that this ability is soon lost as the child grows up, and it is seldom found again!

Therefore, I put the notebooks and drawings away in my attic. Meanwhile, I started reading anything that might lead me to a little understanding of the third-grade children's experiences. Also, I needed time to digest what I had heard and written down. I felt there was something of great importance in these children's experiences, but what it actually was, I wasn't quite sure.

Over the years, I searched through many books, magazines, and newspapers; delved into the lives of past mystics; studied research carried out in the field of parapsychology; examined the lives of many saints; and read and reread the Bible. Slowly, a clearer picture of the stories told by the children started to take form in my mind, and the stories began to make more sense. Perhaps some of the mysteries within them can now be further unraveled.

THE CHILDREN'S REACTIONS

What about the kids? How did they react to all that self-expression during those three years? Well, they enjoyed it! The kids were fascinated by the adventures that happened within themselves and were overjoyed at being able to talk about them. They had plenty of opportunity to express themselves about experiences that nobody else ever listened to or even tried to understand.

These young ones drew pictures, wrote stories, and talked about their experiences in class. They also talked to me privately. Sometimes, I even used a tape recorder and played back their stories to them, and they would laugh at what was going on.

The children were so interested in making drawings of their inner experiences that many times they would ask for extra drawing paper to use during spare moments in school. They would even draw things they saw at home while lying in bed or what they saw happen in church on Sunday. They showed me drawings and told me of their experiences whenever there was a free moment during classes, before school, at noontime, or even after school. They talked and talked, and I listened.

As the teacher of these average, healthy, normal kids, I taught them math, language, and the rest of the regular classroom subjects, but on Friday afternoons our roles were reversed and they taught me things I had never known before. They knew more about their inner experiences than I did, and yet they didn't know themselves what these experiences were really all about. One girl, after having seen what went on inside of her, exclaimed, "I don't believe it, and yet I know it happened!" When they asked me for answers, I didn't know what to tell them because I myself wasn't sure.

The kids gained their own insights into themselves. Anita, a girl who was troubled by voices she kept hearing in the night, said, "I tried to tell these things to my mother, but she wouldn't listen. She would get mad at me and say, 'Stop making up such things! Do you want somebody to think you're crazy?' But in school, since we talked and laughed about hearing voices and other such things, I know that other children also hear and see the same things, and it doesn't bother me anymore. I'm able to think more about my work in school and get better marks. And I feel so much happier!"

The children, when they talked about their experiences, often laughed at what was being said. I laughed with them, at times so hard that tears flowed down my cheeks. However, my laughter was not for the same reasons as theirs. Mine was due to suddenly hearing new insights about another way of life. These children expressed significant revelations that they were not even aware of. They opened up a whole new life for me and made my years in the classroom with them one of the happiest and most exciting periods of my life. They brought me a new understanding of children—one that is entirely different from the one that educators, parents, and authorities on children would have us believe.

These eight-year-olds might have been "mighty prophets," yet they knew it not. Many times, as I listened to them, I felt that perhaps, for the first time in history, they were revealing another story about God and God's world!

GAIL HITS HER HEAD ON THE CEILING

What is the evidence that little children can tell us another story about God?

First, I feel it is important to look at what little children can tell us about psychic phenomena, for we have to know more about such experiences before we can know more about God. A better understanding of psychic phenomena can lead to a better understanding of God.

Modern researchers, as well as those in the past, have tried to unveil the nature of psychic phenomena, but none of them has come up with a clear answer. Scientists of today don't want to accept the psychic aspect of the unknown until they are able to understand how it works. However, the eight-year-old children I taught may have explained how psychic phenomena work better than anyone else has thus far.

For a period of time, I had the young ones imagine how they would solve some of the problems of our troubled world. I liked asking the children their ideas on life to see what they would say. At first, I didn't take their suggestions too seriously. After all, they were only young children. Later on, though, I had to change my mind.

One day the kids were talking about things and I was listening, when, all of a sudden, I heard someone yell, "Ouch!"

I looked over to the side of the room where the yell had come from and saw a girl holding her hand on the top of her head. Gail was the one who had yelled out.

I turned my attention away from the rest of the class to watch Gail for a while as she sat there in her seat with her hand upon her head. A few minutes before, I had seen her with her head down upon her desk, as if she were resting.

"What's the matter, Gail?" I asked.

Gail stood up in the aisle to speak, still holding her hand upon her head. She had a look of pain upon her face. She managed a little grin along with her pain as she said, "I hit my head on the ceiling!"

When the rest of the class heard this, they laughed out loud. Gail, feeling that the other kids were laughing at her for making such a statement, turned to the rest of the class and, stamping her foot on the floor, exclaimed, "I did so!"

I quieted the class, and Gail, a little red in the face, sat down in her seat. Everybody started another assignment they had to do.

A little while later I walked over to where Gail was sitting and asked her very quietly what had happened.

"Well," she said in almost a whisper, "while everyone else was talking, I put my head down on the desk and rested a little. But pretty soon I started to feel myself getting lighter and lighter, and then I saw myself floating up from my seat and toward the ceiling. It was then that my head hit the ceiling, and it hurt. So I hollered, 'Ouch!' "

As a teacher, I had been trying to encourage the children to talk about things they could see in their imaginations, so I talked to Gail a while, quietly, trying to be positive with what I said. Then I went back to my seat while Gail continued her work.

Children are supposed to have good imaginations. However, after years of really listening to children like Gail and then digging into many books, I realized that many of the things they talked about truly did happen.

To my surprise I found a number of books indicating that what had happened to Gail had also happened to others. These books gave an experience such as Gail's a variety of names: "out-of-body experience," "astral projection," or, as people on drugs called it, "taking a trip."

Such an experience is also a way of finding God. While it is happening, the spiritual body separates from the physical body and floats upward toward the ceiling. In most cases, this spiritual body goes right through any obstacle such as a ceiling and then proceeds out into the atmosphere to travel about. However, Gail couldn't get past the ceiling, so she bumped her head on it and then felt it in her physical body below. This made her yell, "Ouch!"

Although Gail didn't mention it, some books claim that the spiritual body and the physical body are still attached during such an experience by means of a cord called an "astral cord" or a "silver cord." Based on my work with the kids, it seems that a truer term for this "cord" would be a "tube," because it is through this tube that feelings can flow between the two bodies. This was why when Gail's spiritual body bumped against the ceiling, she felt it in her physical body that was down below in her seat.

This same experience happened to a well-known saint when she, too, was young. Even as a child, Saint Catherine of Siena was very religious. When she was only six years old, she would go into a cave near her home to pray. While saying her prayers she would suddenly feel herself getting lighter and lighter, and then she would float toward the roof of the cave. She would bang her head against the stone ceiling, and this would bring her out of her trance. This happened to her whenever she said her prayers.

Many people do not know that the spirit body can leave the physical body while a person is still alive. They think this happens only after death. I feel that it can happen in a number of ways while a person is alive and healthy. Some people have even trained themselves to bring this experience on any time they want to.

In most cases, when the spirit body leaves the physical body, it can go right through obstacles like the ceiling of a classroom, as many other children in my classes later said it could. So why, in Gail's case, couldn't she get past the ceiling? And why couldn't Saint Catherine of Siena get past the ceiling of the cave?

An explanation for this is given in a book by scientist Raynor C. Johnson called *The Imprisoned Splendour.* Johnson describes work carried on by a psychic researcher named Yram who was able to project his spirit body out of his physical body with ease. He called his spirit body his "double." He found that his double could be of varying densities, so that under certain conditions a physical object—such as a ceiling—could not be penetrated, while under other conditions he had no trouble passing right through such an obstacle.

MORE OUT-OF-BODY EXPERIENCES

In addition to Gail's experience, various other children in school talked about their "other body" going through the ceiling, moving about in space, and visiting different places. The kids didn't know anything about such things as "out-of-body experiences" or "astral projection" or the spirit body. They referred to such experiences mostly as their "dreams."

What happens when the spirit body leaves the physical body while people are healthy and alive? This can happen, for example, during the process of going to sleep at night. While drifting off to sleep, some people get vague impressions that they are floating upward, but they don't really know what is going on. Then, if a loud bang or noise of some other kind occurs, they may have the impression that they are falling, and wake up with a start. This is caused by the sudden downward movement of the spirit body back into the physical body.

What is the process that occurs when the two bodies separate? Psychic researcher Sylvan Muldoon describes in his book *The Case for Astral Projection* how he trained himself to leave his body anytime he wishes. His physical body remains on his bed while his spirit body travels about. Muldoon claims that he feels fully awake during this process. He later remembers in very clear detail everything he experiences as he moves around outside his body. He can see things and visit places unknown to him and later verify that he has been there.

Consciously separating his two bodies, Muldoon says, is a slow process. When the separation takes place, his spiritual body first floats from three to six feet above his bed and remains in a horizontal position. Then it shifts to a vertical position with a swaying motion. Muldoon says there is an astral cord (as mentioned previously, I call it a tube) linking together his physical head with his spiritual head. This tube is very elastic, exerts a strong pull, and has definite control over his spirit body when his two bodies are within eight to fifteen feet of each other. However, once his spirit body is outside that range, he experiences a feeling of freedom, and his spiritual body can roam wherever his thoughts are concentrated. Nevertheless, the tube is present and visible at all times, even though it becomes very thin as his bodies get farther apart. It can hold this thinness indefinitely.

His spiritual body, Muldoon indicates, is the exact duplicate of his physical body. Sometimes, while he is visiting someone's house in his invisible body, he can pick up things and throw them.

Another researcher, Oliver Fox, wrote in his book *Astral Projection* that while in his spiritual body he sometimes is visible to other people and can carry on a normal conversation with them. However, most of the time he is invisible as he travels about.

There are many adults who have had the mysterious feeling that they have seen or done something before but cannot remember how or when. They are not like Oliver Fox, who can remember the trips he takes. Whether remembered or not, however, the taking of astral flights is a necessary step in the process of traveling to the skies to visit God and the place called heaven, which Emanuel Swedenborg, the famous eighteenth-century mystic, described in his books.

More recent books by Dr. Raymond Moody and Dr. Elisabeth Kübler-Ross explain what happens when the physical body can no longer sustain the spiritual body. In this case there is also an out-of-body experience, but the spiritual body continues to move upward into the heavens, where it remains as part of the "collective unconscious."

AN EIGHT-YEAR-OLD SEES GOD

Is there better evidence for the spiritual experiences of these kids? Did they really say anything about God?

Thomas Carlyle, the famous writer, once stood up in church after listening to a dull sermon and cried out, "What this parish needs, needs before everything else, is a preacher who knows God otherwise than by hearsay. That is the whole world's need."

Some of the children I talked to in school knew God, but they were not preachers. They could not have stood up in church and proclaimed they knew God. However, as a group, they knew more about God than the most knowledgeable theologians in the world today. Their stories described God. Their stories also offered good scientific data on how things happen in the world—information that the scientific world might be interested in hearing!

As Billy Graham once said, "We have pussyfooted long enough in our religion!" Therefore, I will stop pussyfooting around and describe a little girl who met God face-to-face.

During a particular creative expression period, a girl named Jeanne wanted to tell about an experience she had had the night before while in bed, just after she had prayed to God. (Many of the children in the class went to church on Sundays and were well versed in saying their prayers before going to sleep.) However, the period was just about over and there was little time for her to talk, so Jeanne stayed after all the other children had gone home and came up to my desk with a paper in her hand.

"I have a drawing I want to show you," Jeanne said, placing her paper in the middle of my desk. (See plate 1.)

I looked at Jeanne's drawing the way I had looked at hundreds of children's drawings. I always tried to figure out what they meant, but most of the time I met with little success. Usually what the children drew was far beyond my understanding. They saw so many things inside their invisible world that if their experiences had not been captured on paper, they would soon have been forgotten, because new experiences would have moved in to take their place.

In this instance, Jeanne's drawing looked simple enough to understand. I asked her, as I usually did, "So, what happened here?"

"It happened last night in bed." Jeanne said. "I was sort of half awake and half asleep when suddenly up in the sky I was able to see a blue, wavy line come down, and it came right toward me and went into my body."

"How did it get into your body?" I asked.

"It came into my head first. Then it went down one side, going into my right arm and down to my right leg. Then it went over to the other side, to my left foot, up to my left arm, and then back up to my head."

"How could you tell that was happening?" I asked.

"I felt the line doing that, and I could see it."

"Do you mean you could see the line moving like that inside your body?"

"That's right," Jeanne said. "I could see it inside my body."

"How can you see inside your body?"

"I don't know, but I did. Then the line went down into my heart. When this happened, red, wavy lines started to come out of my body, all around me. I could see them. Then one red, wavy line banged into another red, wavy line, and this made sparks fly, and then there was a 'bang,' like an explosion, making a flash of light. This seemed to explode all the other red lines around me, and the next thing I knew there was a bright yellow light around my whole body!"

I was so amazed at what Jeanne was saying that I just sat there, staring at her drawing, not knowing what to say next. Finally I asked, "Did anything else happen?"

"Yes, there was more," Jeanne said, "but I'm not sure I can explain it. There were some red, wavy lines inside my head that were still trying to get out, but the yellow light that was still all around me was pushing in, and the red lines couldn't get out. The red lines kept trying and trying to get out but couldn't. The next thing I knew, I was floating toward the ceiling. I looked down, and there was my other body—still lying on the bed."

Jeanne stopped talking at this point. She stood there looking down at her drawing, and I sat there at my desk also looking down at her drawing. What could I say to an eight-year-old child who had just told me such a story? Should I say that it was all nonsense? That she was making the whole thing up? I couldn't do that. She had told the story in such a confident manner that I felt somehow that she knew what she was talking about. However, it seemed like I should say something, so I asked her, "What happened next?"

"Next," Jeanne said, "I seemed to go right through the ceiling, through the roof of the house and out into the night. And I went to different places. The first person I thought of was my friend Carol, and the next thing I knew I was there. I saw Carol inside her house, but she didn't seem to be able to see me. I tried to get her attention but couldn't. I even went inside her body, but she didn't seem to know what was going on. Pretty soon I left, and that's all that happened there."

Jeanne had more she wanted to tell me, but I was so shaken up by what she had already said that I wanted to walk down the hall, get a drink, and perhaps recover a little from the amazing story she had just told. Jeanne said she would wait until I came back.

When I returned to the room, Jeanne was still there, waiting to tell me more about what happened while her spiritual body was out of her physical body. After she moved away from Carol's house, her thoughts returned to her prayer and wish to visit God.

"Just as I had those thoughts," Jeanne said, "I started moving upward, higher and higher into the sky, until finally I came to a cloud—a shining, yellow cloud. I couldn't see anything because I was right in the middle of the cloud. Then a hand reached down and took my hand. At that instant I felt a great joy fill my body. I didn't know why until later. The hand led me up two flights of stairs. Then the yellow cloud cleared, and I could see a golden castle, and it was God who was holding my hand!"

"What happened next?" I asked, again becoming quite dazed by what Jeanne was telling me.

"I was able to look around. There were angels all over. Jesus was there, and I talked to God just as I'm talking to you. And I talked to Jesus, too."

"How did God and Jesus look to you?" I asked, uncertain about what to ask her.

"I could see them both dressed in beautifully colored gowns," Jeanne said. "The yellow light that filled heaven, which was below, came from God. God's gown was also gold in color. Jesus and God both had long hair. Jesus had rounded cheeks and looked younger, while God had thin cheeks and looked much older."

That was all Jeanne had to say, so she left to go home. I just sat there, alone, not wanting to move, as my mind raced over the things this girl had told me. Tears started streaming down my face as my thoughts turned to the Bible. I realized it might be true that the pure of heart shall be able to see God, for a child who was only eight years old surely must have a heart that is still pure. I also felt that there was truth in the Bible's comment that unless we become as little children, we shall not enter the kingdom of heaven.

Eventually, the tears stopped flowing down my cheeks, and I went home.

IN SEARCH OF THE TRUTH

Could Jeanne's story have been true? Her account of what happened to her was one of the best and most complete that these young and seemingly innocent children told me. Usually I heard only little pieces of information at a time. With my adult mind, I had to put the pieces together in a way that seemed like they might fit.

As mentioned in the previous chapter, I found that the things children were able to see in their private, inner worlds were soon gone and mostly forgotten. New images and experiences would quickly move in to take their place. This is where I came in: to hear what the children had to say, to have them draw pictures of what they saw, and to help them capture some of the things that happened to them shortly after they took place—things I had never even known could really happen, things of which the adult world was not even aware.

Most of the experiences the children told me did not reflect the beliefs of a particular religion—they were just events in the daily lives of young children. Such experiences, if they had happened to an adult rather than a child, might have lead to the formation of a new religion!

The chapters that follow will provide evidence to support the story told by Jeanne. This evidence depicts a very different picture of life on Earth than the one we hold as valid today.

ATTUNING THE HUMAN BODY
"I was sort of half awake and half asleep . . ."

Jeanne's experience began when she was half asleep. She was still awake, but she had begun moving toward the sleep stage. At some point in the period of time between waking and sleeping she was able to come into visual contact with God's world.

Such a period of time, during which a state of equilibrium develops, is a key factor in the occurrence of mystical experiences. Such a period represents a state of balance in which one force moves toward what might be called a "zero point" before an opposite force starts to take over. A state of equilibrium is a stopping point in a transition between any opposite factors. It creates a feeling of "nothingness" within the body. It is during such a state that the spiritual body can leave the physical body or that a person can have similar spiritual experiences.

Emanuel Swedenborg commented on such an experience in one of his many writings: "It was my spirit that journeyed, while my body remained in the same place." He also described how such an event happens: "When a man is withdrawn from the body and his spirit is carried away to another place, it first starts under certain conditions, and it is this—in a state of being which is halfway between sleeping and waking—and when in that state he appears to be wide awake, and can remember everything with such clarity as in being fully awake."

Attuning the human body may come naturally to young children. Such an attunement to God's force might even be given a name that psychologists have used more often in the past: instinct. It is a behavior pattern that the "authorities" as yet do not understand. I feel, however, that this state involves a continuous influx of spiritual forces into the bodies of young children.

Children, as they grow up, gradually lose this attunement to spiritual forces. After about eight years of age, they begin shifting away from these forces and start developing reasoning powers. As adults, people try to recapture this ability again through religion, meditation, drugs, sex, and so on.

As far as I have learned, however, young children can provide the most detailed information on how God and God's world might operate. The equilibrium that is needed in the body to make contact with forces from above can occur in children very quickly, even when they are in bed half asleep. It can also happen to them after they say a prayer in church, or when they put their heads down on their school desks, breathe deeply several times, relax their bodies, and think of God. If conditions are right, a child in a public school classroom can make this contact with God in about ten to fifteen seconds.

Yogis, with their meditation techniques, sitting positions, and deep breathing, go through long periods of training to develop such an attunement or state of equilibrium for making contact with the forces from above. Other adults generally experience difficulty in trying to reach the state of equilibrium required to make contact with God. As it says in the Bible, we have to be "born again" and "become as little children" in order to make such a contact.

WHAT ARE THE VIBRATIONS?
"I was able to see a blue, wavy line come down . . ."

Jeanne said a prayer in which she spoke to God above. After her prayer, a force came down from high in the sky in the form of a vibration. Jeanne referred to it as a "wavy line." Being only eight years old, she probably was not acquainted with the term "vibration."

According to Jeanne, God responded from someplace in the sky, and God's powers moved down in the form of this vibration. According to other children I talked to, God's power can move down in a variety of ways. However, for Jeanne, this power came as a blue vibration.

What is the nature of the wavy line that God sent down to this little girl? I have never read or heard of anyone else who has been able to give a good description of such a colored vibration. Many people on Earth don't even know that such vibrations exist. A few adults are familiar with them in a vague sort of way, but they know very little about them. The children, however, could actually see these vibrations with their special type of vision. They could also see them moving both outside and inside their bodies.

According to the children, the forces from above moved not only as vibrations, but also as spirals and lines. A force might have manifested as a big, powerful spiral, similar to the whirlwinds mentioned in the Bible, or as a straight line.

Based on the children's experiences, the two basic movements of the God force inside the body were a wavy motion on one side of the body and a zigzag motion on the other side of the body. The wavy vibration moved along inside the body very easily and was hardly noticed. However, the zigzag formation, as one girl said, "moved along just under the skin, and where the points of the line reached the skin, it gave me a prickly feeling!"

These two movements of the powers of God inside a living thing may be the basis for all life on Earth, reflecting the positive and negative electrical forces of life. These two movements may also explain the male and female forms of life, as I will discuss later.

For these children, the spiritual force descended primarily as a single vibration. However, sometimes there were two vibrations that descended side by side, or a cluster of different-colored lines that came down together. The lines would enter the children's bodies mainly through the tops of their heads and then circle around inside their bodies. Sometimes they would also pass out of their bodies through their hands or feet.

Such vibrations may be one way for God to contact people on Earth directly. They seem to appear first as empty tubes, if the participants are watching closely enough. Then, as one girl said, "This tube seems to grow longer and longer at the tip." After the tubes are formed, colors are able to flow through them.

What Jeanne saw was a glowing blue vibration coming down from above to enter her body. Other children told of seeing vibrations in a variety of colors, particularly those of which white light is composed—red, orange, yellow, green, blue, and purple—but no brown or black. Several children described heaven, the area above where God was located, as being made up of white light.

What is the nature of these colors? The best description I could get from the children was that the colors were composed of a fluid of some kind that flowed like a liquid—yet was not a liquid. This fluid seemed to be a flow of glowing energy that moved along inside the tubes and gave off light. Sometimes sparks were seen, as if it were a flow of electricity that had been made visible. Also, this fluid seemed to have the properties of being alive; it had an intelligence to it.

The tubes seen by these children, filled with different-colored fluids, might have been the same as those experienced by the mystics of the Far East, who described channels filled with psychic energies that flowed through the body. Such tubes, following regular channels, may also be responsible for the ability of some people to cure sickness by what is called "laying on of hands." This is a process by which healers cure other people's illnesses simply by placing their hands upon the affected areas. It is my belief that these healers have the God force flowing through their bodies in the form of these vibrations. Perhaps each vibration of a different color carries a particular characteristic of the God force and so causes a different reaction within the human body. One colored fluid may cause the body to become "whole" again. Another may cause a feeling of great spiritual love. Yet another may cause a feeling of great joy, and so on. These vibrating tubes may be able to come out of the fingertips of a healer and move into another person's body.

One girl in school was able to see these colored vibrations coming out of her fingers, and she turned in a drawing that may possibly show the vibrational activity within a hand that heals. (See plate 2.)

THE INTELLIGENCE WITHIN THE VIBRATIONS
". . . it came right toward me and went into my body."

After Jeanne's prayer, God responded with a flow of force in the form of a blue vibration. This force went directly to the girl as she lay in bed, and then it entered her body. The flow of blue substance seemed to have an intelligence to it. As another girl said, "When it happened to me, it acted like it had a mind of its own and seemed to know what it was doing—as if it were a living thing."

We are told that God is omnipresent, that is, God can be at different places at the same time. But we do not know how this is possible. It may be that flows of substance coming down from above are extensions of God. Such extensions may be only single slender vibrations, as Jeanne saw, or broad bands of energy descending like winds (as others have seen them), or flames of light (as in other reports).

They Walked with God, edited by Michael Williams, recounts a story about Saint Francis of Assisi and his encounter with a light from above. One night while he was kneeling and praying to God, his face and hands raised toward heaven, a bright light that was like a flame of fire descended and landed upon his head. Out of this flame, a voice spoke to him. After awhile, the light rose back into the sky. Later on, when Saint Francis was asked about the incident, he said that he had seen God in the flame.

It is said that the Christian world is waiting for Jesus to return to Earth. If we were to listen carefully to children, we might realize that some children are able to see Jesus now, as children probably have been able to see him in times past.

Gail, the girl who had bumped her head on the ceiling, described how a spiritual force came down from above, went through her body, and then changed into a spiritual person from heaven. Unlike Saint Francis, it wasn't God whom Gail saw—it was Jesus. Based on her story, it seems that it may be possible for the force belonging to a spiritual individual to move along a vibration, perhaps at the speed of light, and then at its destination revert into the form of the spiritual individual again.

When the Lord's Prayer was said before morning classes, school regulations prohibited any comments being made about its meaning or about what was being felt or experienced by anyone. However, during the special creative expression period, I was allowed to see or hear whatever any child wanted to express.

Therefore, during one of these Friday afternoon periods, I asked the children in the class to bow their heads and say the Lord's Prayer as they did every morning before classtime, if they wanted to. They were to watch what happened—if anything—and to write it down or draw a picture of what they saw.

A few children had things to say about the prayer, and they stood up and talked about it. I also watched Gail to see if she would do any talking, because things usually happened to her when she bowed her head to pray. However, Gail did not like to talk in front of the other children; she was quite shy, and sometimes the others would laugh a little at the things she said.

Later on, when the rest of the class was working on their drawings, I caught Gail's eye and gave her a signal to come up to my desk where we could talk more privately. She came up with a drawing in her hand. (See figure 1.)

Gail started talking in a low voice because she did not want the other children to hear her. She said, "When I had my hands together and was saying the Lord's Prayer, I suddenly was able to see a line come down from the sky, and it came right toward me."

"What kind of a line?" I asked.

"I don't know," Gail said, "but the line came right at me."

Gail did not know it yet, but such a line, examined closely by other children, was actually a slender tube through which spiritual fluids flowed. She went on to describe how the line entered her head and then moved around inside her, first traveling down one side of her body and then going up the other side. After doing this, it circled her body a second time and then left her body and went up into the air.

"When this happened," Gail said, "I started to see a white light shining inside my body. It was brightest inside my chest, and a wonderful feeling came all over and inside of me."

Gail became excited as she talked, and her voice got louder. She suddenly looked out over the classroom to make sure the other children were not listening to her. They were all busy with their own work, so she went on with her story. "Something else happened later on. It was after seeing that shining white light inside of me that I looked up and could see heaven, high up in the sky. Then heaven seemed to open up, and another line started coming down, like before."

"Can you tell me anything about the line?" I asked, not knowing what to ask her about the white light.

"I can't say much about the line," Gail said, "except that it had

Figure 1. How Jesus Was Seen on Earth. *Gail, an eight-year-old child, said the Lord's Prayer quietly to herself. Shortly after that, a force like electricity came down from the sky and entered her body. After making three stops, it came out her toes. Then it whirled around in front of her. From this Jesus appeared and talked to Gail. This caused a great joy to fill her body!*

big wiggles in it as it came down, and it came right at me again. It came into my head first and then went down my body, and it felt like bolts of lightning!"

"What do you mean, 'bolts of lightning'?" I asked, becoming more alert to such a comment.

"It felt like electricity going through me," she said. "And it stopped inside my body at three different places. It went down as far as my stomach and stopped. Then it went down to my knee and stopped. And then it went into my toes and stopped again."

"What happened then?" I asked.

"The line came out of my toes," she answered.

Gail went on, telling me about things in this other world that I knew very little about: "And as it came out of my toes, it turned upward and then stopped right there in front of me!"

Gail paused only for a moment and then continued. "The line didn't really stop, but went into a spin—right there in front of me. It whirled around and around and around, like a big ball of light. And then where the spinning was going on, the figure of a person started to form right there in front of me! It was the figure of a man. And then I recognized who he was. It was Jesus! I had seen him before, and so I knew him."

"And?" I asked, too dazed to be able to say anything more.

"We talked awhile," Gail continued, "and every word that Jesus spoke seemed to go right through me, and it made a very happy feeling all over and inside of me."

"Anything else?" I asked limply, staring at the drawing she had put on my desk. Gail didn't talk for awhile—she just kept looking down at her drawing. Finally, she concluded by saying that Jesus had left after talking with her, moving back up into the sky along the same vibration on which he had come down and which Gail said she could still see in the sky. The line disappeared behind him as he moved back toward heaven.

If other people had been watching Gail while she was having this experience, they probably would not have seen anything. What happened to her took place within the spiritual world, which usually is invisible to others. This is mentioned by Swedenborg, who said that a person "in the spirit," as it is called in the Bible, can see what takes place in the spiritual world, but that another person present will usually see nothing.

How do we know that Gail's experience truly happened? Well, many factors checked out. Gail's body turned white, especially in the chest area. This phenomenon has been described in books on the Tibetan mystics. Also, the vibration coming down from the sky and then circling about inside her was something frequently mentioned by other children. The whirling action of the spiritual force was another key factor that other children talked about.

When Gail had the conversation with Jesus, the rest of us in the classroom were not able to see her lips move because such a conversation takes place with thoughts only, according to Swedenborg. Therefore, Gail did not have to move her lips or talk out loud.

Gail's story, accompanied by her drawing, was one of the best accounts I heard from the children on the ability of a spiritual being to flow along a vibration in the form of a spiritual substance and, later on, change back into a spiritual personality. In this case, the spiritual being was Jesus. In the same manner, we could be in communication with God!

This phenomenon may be related to Einstein's famous formula $E=mc^2$, or $mc^2=E$: mass (a spiritual person) is converted into energy (spiritual energy) that flows as a vibration of light. In the spiritual world, this formula may be reversible and so move in either direction.

A THEORY OF LIFE
"It came into my head first."

Why not try to develop a theory of life on Earth? Others have tried it, and, according to the things I heard from the kids in class, the others' theories seem to be on the right track. Put their theories all together and we may have something close to the whole truth.

In Jeanne's experience, a force came down from above, entered her body through one side of her head, went down the same side of her body, crossed over to the other half of her body, and then went back up to the other side of her head, as if to complete a circuit. I heard this description many times from the children.

An explanation for this circular flow of force may offer a clue to the origin of life on Earth. This explanation, I feel, has to do with the two opposite, yet complementary, characteristics of the force that comes from God: the positive and the negative. These complementary aspects of the spiritual force are the same as the positive and negative aspects of the electrical force.

It seems that the human body's right side has a positive electrical charge, while the left side has a negative electrical charge. When the God force enters the body, it moves in a manner that completes a circuit in the body.

The various philosophies of the world all present the idea of complementary aspects of a spiritual force, but with different names for this dual force of God. Sometimes it is called the male-female force. Other times it is called the sun-moon force. In the Chinese yang-yin theory of life, yang represents the male force and yin the female force. Both work together in harmony.

Swedenborg, in his writings, used the word "correspondence" when he stated that what is in heaven corresponds to what we see on Earth. The physical sun that we see by day and the physical moon that we see by night correspond to the spiritual sun and spiritual moon representing God above. (Another concept of God, the "God beyond God," will be discussed later.)

According to Swedenborg, there is a spiritual influx of energy from God that enters all people on Earth. The influx of this God force into children may be different from the influx into adults. Children can receive both the male and female forces at the same time. Then, as they reach adolescence, a change takes place within their bodies so that males receive only the male force and females receive only the female force. This causes a rapid maturation of the sex organs in the period that follows.

As young people continue to grow, they experience the normal urge to unite with the opposite sex. The experience of physical love completes the circuit of the spiritual positive and negative current moving through their bodies.

The flow of current through a person's body may determine his or her male or female characteristics. In the male body, the current may flow only in a clockwise direction, while in the female body it may flow only in the opposite direction—counterclockwise. In certain people, however, this flow of current may not follow the normal pattern. The flow may reverse itself, causing a male person to develop feminine tendencies or a female person to develop masculine tendencies. This is speculation on my part, and more research is needed to see if this idea has some basis in fact.

The expression "God is love" may not be true, according to what I heard the children say. Perhaps a more accurate way of expressing this sentiment would be to say that from God there is an energy influx into the body that can cause the feeling of love. The adult male, when he is able to make contact with God, receives into his body the female force. As this moves through his body, completing the male-female electrical circuit within him, it causes a feeling that could be called "spiritual love." This spiritual love is likewise experienced by the adult female who receives into her body the male God force. This is what the mystics, as well as other people who have had encounters with God, experience as "ecstasy."

Books about the mystics say that the highest state a person can reach in his or her spiritual search is the ability to unite the male and female forces within the body. When this happens, the "sacred fire" of enlightenment springs up within the person. This force grows and grows, producing a great internal heat along with a spiritual feeling of love. This is known as the "yoga of the inner fire."

The sacred writings of the Jewish people, as found in the holy Cabala, describe a man's need of the female force in order to complete life. This female force could come from a wife on Earth as well as from God above.

What has this to do with little children in a public school? What do they know about the mystics? Or the holy Cabala? Or about the yin-yang theory of life? How much would children know about such ideas on life? Nothing. Yet they had a lot to say about such matters.

PIAGET AND THE CHILD

The old Tibetan mystics claimed that there were two main channels of energy flowing through the human body. On the right side of the body, they said, a "sun" force flows, while on the left side a "moon" force flows.

Swedenborg stated that people who are "in the spirit" can see God with their right eyes as a sun shining in the sky and with their left eyes as a moon. This again is the concept that the God-force is dual in nature: positive-negative, male-female, and sun-moon.

It also suggests a basis for a few of the ideas found in astrology. The sun and moon mentioned in astrology are the sun and moon that we normally see above us in the sky. However, it is the spiritual sun and spiritual moon, which together create the God force, that may actually influence us. Therefore, astrologers may interpret the courses of the physical sun and moon in a spiritual way.

Children's drawings often portray a sun shining in the sky. As Swedenborg said, the right eye sees God as a sun, and that is the way some of the children in my classes said they saw God. Ancient people believed that the spiritual sun in the sky was God— and they may have been right!

Jean Piaget, the noted child psychologist, found that many children spoke about the sun and moon (*The New York Times Magazine*, May 26, 1968). He said that children, when they were out walking, claimed to see the sun and moon following them about. Piaget listened to the children very carefully and was completely objective, but he did not come to any conclusions about their comments. He was interested mainly in how the children reasoned.

There are some child psychologists today who may be presenting incorrect information to the general public. They do not really know what goes on inside children. They listen to children and then try to form conclusions based on the thinking of their own adult minds. However, their thinking may be altogether different from what goes on in the minds of children, so the conclusions they reach may be far from the truth. As Dr. Maria Montessori, founder of the noted schools that bear her name, stated in her book *The Secret of Childhood,* "The psychology of children has been studied from the adult rather than from a child's point of view. As a consequence, their conclusions must be radically reviewed!"

A little girl named Teresa drew a picture of the sun and moon that she saw quite often overhead as she walked back and forth to school. In her picture was a force that she saw come down from the sky one day. It came to her from the sun, circled inside her body several times, and then returned into the sky to the moon. (See figure 2.)

THE OLD MAN WHO WASN'T THERE

"The first person I thought of was my friend Carol,
and the next thing I knew I was there."

Children do not know the power of thought. Even adults do not know the power of their own thinking, so how would an eight-year-old girl? Jeanne thought of Carol, and the next instant her spirit body was with her friend, who lived about two miles away.

It seems that moving through space in the spiritual world is an amazingly rapid feat. A few adults have written about traveling in the spiritual world. They have even visited foreign countries within a matter of a few seconds, which would involve moving at almost the speed of light! Swedenborg actually wrote about visiting heaven in his spirit body and then coming back to Earth to write about it.

How thought can do this to the spirit body, I do not know, but thought seems to have great power under the right conditions. The mystics of the Far East can use their thoughts to bring spiritual people into being. Other people can also see these spiritual beings or thoughtforms. Madame Alexandra David-Neel, a French Buddhist, writes in her book *Magic and Mystery* in Tibet about one such created person, whom she calls a "tulpa."

Madame David-Neel, an expert on the ways of the yogis, knew about the tulpas created by the mystics with their thoughts and wanted to create such an imaginary person for herself. Using great powers of concentration, she was able after a time to bring a short,

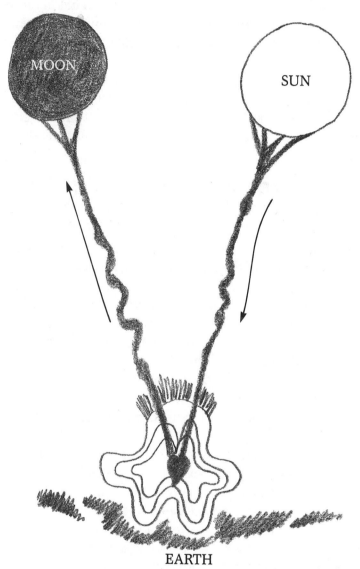

EARTH

Figure 2. The Sun and Moon Theory of Life. *One day as Teresa was walking home from school, she saw the Sun and Moon overhead. Then suddenly she saw a force come down from the Sun, go through her body several times, and return into the sky to the Moon.*

jolly lama into being. He was seen by other people at various times and seemed to be a real person. After a while, however, this tulpa started to develop a mean personality, which annoyed Madame David-Neel. It then took a great effort on her part to dissipate the energies that had created him in the first place and so put an end to him.

Without realizing it, children seem similarly able to manifest spiritual beings, and they can do so within a short period of time. Also, they don't need any training, as do the mystics. To children, this ability is a normal, natural fact of life.

For instance, one child in class told me that when she thought of a certain person she started to see colored particles in the atmosphere start moving toward her. Her thoughts seemed to act like a magnet, drawing together in front of her the round balls of a colored substance belonging to the person she was thinking of. Finally she would see that person standing in front of her, as if in real life. This would occur in the spiritual world, of course, and no one else would be able to see the person. (See plate 3.)

Many mothers hear about the friends their children claim to have whom no one else sees. To children, who can see into the spiritual world, their friends are very real. These friends are brought into being just by the power of the children's thoughts.

There are certain conditions that tend to enhance this ability. One is that a child be alone quite often. Another is that his or her thoughts be concentrated on a particular person or being. A third is that a strong emotion be present, which can help speed things up.

For one girl in class named Lorna, the emotion that brought an image of a person into being for her was fear. However, she didn't know what her experience was all about.

One day I asked the children if anything had ever happened to them that seemed strange or that they couldn't understand. Nobody in class said anything for awhile, and I was just about to go on with our regular classroom work when Lorna raised her hand.

"Something did happen to me once," Lorna said, "and I haven't been able to figure it out. It was about an old man that I saw, and then he disappeared right before my eyes!"

There wasn't much time for discussion right then, so I told Lorna that when she had some spare time during the day we would talk some more. Later, Lorna finished an assignment early and came up to my desk to tell me more about what had happened.

One Saturday morning, Lorna's family was preparing to go into town to do some shopping. Lorna lived in the country on a dirt road, in a house that was by itself, away from any other houses. That morning she was to stay at home and take care of things. Although she was only eight years old, she was left at home quite often. Lorna didn't mind this—in fact, she liked staying home alone.

As her mother was going out the door, she yelled back to Lorna, "Remember, if the old man comes to the house, don't let him in."

The old man lived alone up the road a distance. No one knew anything about him except that he said "fresh things" to people, and it was believed that he had lots of money. He had a long beard, and blue eyes that seemed to look right through people.

After the family left, Lorna settled down on the couch with a book. The house was pleasantly quiet, but after a while it seemed too quiet to Lorna, and the stillness started to bother her a little. She looked around for Rusty, the family dog, for a little companionship, but didn't see him anywhere. "He must be outside," she said half-aloud to herself.

Lorna kept reading her book, but her uneasiness grew. Her thoughts turned to the last words her mother had said: "If the old man comes to the house, don't let him in."

Suddenly, fear overcame Lorna. What if the old man did come? What should she do? She looked around some more for the dog, wishing he was there with her, but again realized that he must be outside.

By now Lorna had lost interest in reading, so she just sat still, not thinking about anything special. However, the old man kept creeping into her thoughts, scaring her more and more.

"Then I heard a noise at the door," Lorna told me. "It was as if someone was there. Most of the time it's the dog scratching at the door, wanting to come in. But this time I wasn't sure. So I got up from the couch and went over and opened the door, and there stood the old man!"

Lorna didn't know what to do. The sudden sight of the figure in the doorway petrified her. She just stood there looking at the old man, unable to move. The old man also stood still, staring down at her with his blue, penetrating eyes.

Lorna felt she should say something, but she didn't know what. Finally she managed to exclaim, "Won't you please come in?" This was the one thing she was not supposed to say.

The old man, with his long beard and blue eyes, continued to stare down at her awhile more and then said, "No, I have to go."

The old man turned around and headed down the walkway toward the road. When he had gone about ten feet, Lorna's great fear suddenly left her. Then, as Lorna later explained to me, "An odd thing happened. When that old man was about ten feet away, he suddenly disappeared! Right before my eyes! It looked like he came apart, and the different parts of his body drifted off into the air! This is the part I don't understand. Where did he go?"

I, her teacher, didn't know where the old man went. At that time I didn't understand the phenomenon myself. However, as I look back at Lorna's story now, I realize that her experience could have been similar to the materialization accomplished by Madame David-Neel.

There were several key conditions present that would have allowed the old man to materialize for Lorna as a spirit being who appeared similar to his actual physical self. As Lorna's mother went out the door, she reminded Lorna not to let the old man into the house if he came by. This last comment was left for Lorna to think about, and she did think about it. In fact, as she sat alone in the quietness of the house her thoughts became more and more concentrated on the old man, and fear began creeping in. Three conditions key to the manifestation of a spirit being were therefore present: solitude, a concentration of thought on a particular individual, and the emotion of fear, which further increased the power of the thought concentration.

The old man himself was probably minding his own business

somewhere else, not concerned at all about the little girl who lived down the road. However, because he had walked the dirt road that passed Lorna's house many times, his physical body may have radiated energy from his spiritual body that was lingering in the vicinity. Lorna, not realizing the power of her thoughts, may have been able to draw together enough of this energy from the old man to create a spiritual manifestation of him. The next thing she knew there was a noise at the door, and when she opened the door, there stood the old man. He even looked like the real thing, with his long beard and his blue, penetrating eyes.

Fear of the old man was still in Lorna as she talked to him. However, as the old man turned around and walked away, Lorna's fear suddenly left her. At that instant, the old man started to disintegrate. As Lorna said, "It looked like he came apart, and the different parts of his body drifted off into the air!" Probably, that's exactly what happened. The fear that had gripped Lorna had helped form the image of the old man, and the release of that fear was enough for the spiritual particles of the old man to be set free again. They probably drifted back to where they had been before Lorna had pulled them together. This is what I believe happened.

Lorna's process was probably similar to that experienced by the girl who drew the picture in plate 3. It was probably also the same as that experienced by Madame Alexandra David-Neel.

As alluded to previously, a thought, in the spiritual world, seems to act like a magnet, able to pull together the energies belonging to a certain person and therefore make that person appear as if he or she were physically present.

A DEPARTED GRANDMOTHER RETURNS

William Blake, the noted English artist, poet, and mystic, described people in his works whom he saw in the spirit world. He began seeing these spiritual beings at the age of eight, when his younger brother, Robert, passed away. For years afterward, Blake talked to his brother in the spirit world almost every day.

I mentioned in the previous chapter that wherever a human being moves about on Earth, spiritual particles from them remain for some time. Through deep, concentrated thought, another person may be able to pull those particles together again, and so manifest the original person.

Similarly, a departed person who now resides as a living spirit in heaven may be brought back to Earth by someone in the physical plane if conditions are right. Some of these conditions were mentioned in the previous chapter. One condition is that the person on the physical plane be alone for a period of time. Another is that he or she think often about the departed person. Also, his or her physical body needs to be in a relaxed state. There may be other conditions, but these are enough to make things happen.

One morning in school, the bell had rung for the start of the first-period class, and the children were busy with written work that was supposed to be completed as soon as possible. All of them were working except Elaine. When I looked at her, there was a sad expression on her face and a faraway look in her eyes.

Perhaps, I thought, there was something wrong and I should talk to her. But thinking that she might soon start her work, I waited awhile. She continued to just sit there. Finally I called her up to my desk.

"Is anything wrong, Elaine?" I asked in a quiet voice.

Elaine didn't say anything for awhile. Then she said in a low, subdued voice, "I feel so sad."

"What's there to be sad about?"

"I miss my grandmother," she said.

"Where is your grandmother?"

"She used to live with us. She visited me yesterday and that made me happy. Then she went away, and that's why I'm sad."

"Where does she live now?" I asked.

Elaine moved in closer to my desk and, in a voice that I could hardly hear, said, "My grandmother is dead. She died over a year ago. But sometimes she comes back to visit. She came back yesterday and then she left, and that makes me sad."

Elaine was an only child, and both her father and mother worked. When she had arrived home the day before, her house had been empty. She had felt so lonesome that she had gone up to her bedroom, the one her grandmother had slept in when she was alive.

Elaine went on in her low voice: "I now have the room my grandmother used to have. Before, when the house was quiet and no one was home after school, I'd go up to the bedroom and sit down in the rocking chair I used to sit in when my grandmother was alive. I'd pull Granny's rocker, which was still in the room, over next to mine, and I'd just sit there thinking of her.

Pretty soon I would hear light footsteps coming up the stairs. The bedroom door would be open, and the steps would come into the room, and I'd feel that someone had come into the room and had sat down in the chair next to mine. I wouldn't be able to see anything yet. I'd believe that it was Granny's spirit that had come back. In Sunday school I asked the teacher questions, and she said that the body of a person passes away but the spirit stays alive. I never told her what I saw, but only asked questions so that I could understand things better. The next thing I would do would be to start talking as if Granny were there. Pretty soon I would be able to see her sitting there as if she were really there; she would even be wearing the same clothes she had on when I last saw her alive.

"But yesterday, as I was sitting in the rocking chair and thinking of Granny, I saw her come down from heaven in a wavy motion." Elaine made a motion with her hand to show how her grandmother descended. "I could see just the outline of her body at first, as she came right toward me. She came into the room and sat down in her chair. In a little while she appeared as she looked in real life.

"We talked for awhile," Elaine continued. "I'm always so very happy when we talk, for it makes me remember the good times we had together. When Granny couldn't do things, I would help her. Sometimes I would talk too much. Then I would hear a voice in my mind say, 'Stop it!' And I'd stop and listen to what Granny had to say. As she was sitting there yesterday, she had her arm on the side of the rocker, and I reached over to put my hand on her arm, but it passed right through her arm, and all I was touching was the wood on the chair. Then I realized that Granny was there only in spirit. When my mind thought of this, my grandmother disappeared, and that's why I'm so sad today, because I miss her so."

After this long period of talking, Elaine didn't seem to have anything else to say. A short while later, she shrugged her shoulders, gave a slight grin, and went back to her seat and started her classwork.

About two months later, I asked Elaine if she was still seeing her grandmother. "I haven't seen her lately," Elaine said. "But the other day I saw my mother go dashing up the stairs. Later, when I asked my mother what was the matter, she said that she thought she heard Granny calling from upstairs and hurried up to see if she was there."

Conditions were right for Elaine's grandmother to have materialized. Each time it happened, Elaine first felt that her grandmother was present, but she could not see her. Then, as time went by and her concentration increased, the spiritual substance that made up her grandmother's spiritual body was probably pulled together strongly enough by Elaine's thoughts to cause her grandmother to appear.

Evidence that this event actually occurred was the wavy motion that Elaine described. A wavy pathway extending downward from above is the route taken by most spiritual energies, and Elaine probably would never have mentioned such a vibration if it hadn't happened.

The power of Elaine's thoughts was particularly apparent when she went to put her hand on her grandmother's arm. Her hand went right through the arm without feeling it, and instead she found herself holding the wood of the rocking chair. At that point her thinking changed, and she realized that her grandmother was not really there as a physical person. The power of her thoughts about her grandmother was therefore weakened, allowing her grandmother's spiritual particles to come apart and dissipate. Her grandmother then vanished!

COSMIC CONSCIOUSNESS
".. . there was a bright yellow light around my whole body!"

Only a few people, great people of the past, were supposed to have experienced "cosmic consciousness." During this experience, God and the person were united, causing the person's body to be surrounded by a golden glow and the person to be filled with a great joy or ecstasy.

Richard Bucke's *Cosmic Consciousness* is considered a classic on this subject. The author had a cosmic-consciousness experience himself, and it led him to study the lives of great people of the past who had encountered the same thing. Those he studied included Saint Augustine, Spinoza, Buddha, Dante, William Blake, and Walt Whitman. Muhammad, the founder of Islam, also had a cosmic-consciousness experience.

Dr. Bucke, writing about his own experience, said, "All at once, without warning, I found myself wrapped in a flame-colored cloud. For an instant I thought of fire, the next, I knew that the fire was within myself."

Today, people are searching for the cause of such experiences.

Children may experience bright light around their bodies more often than we realize. Jeanne, as she lay in bed, saw a bright yellow light surrounding her body and later gave me a pretty good explanation of how it happened. She was able to see sparks fly when one vibration touched another vibration. These sparks set off a chain reaction, igniting all the other vibrations and causing the bright yellow glow to form around her whole body. Whether Jeanne experienced ecstasy in her encounter with God she did not say, as other things were happening quickly at the time.

Another girl named Diane, however, told me about seeing a bright light around her body, and she did experience the great joy, or ecstasy, that is supposed to accompany it. She came up to my desk with a drawing one day during the last period and said, "This is what I saw happen to me last Sunday in church." (See figure 3.)

"Do you want to explain your drawing?" I asked.

Diane said that after saying a prayer in church she felt sort of

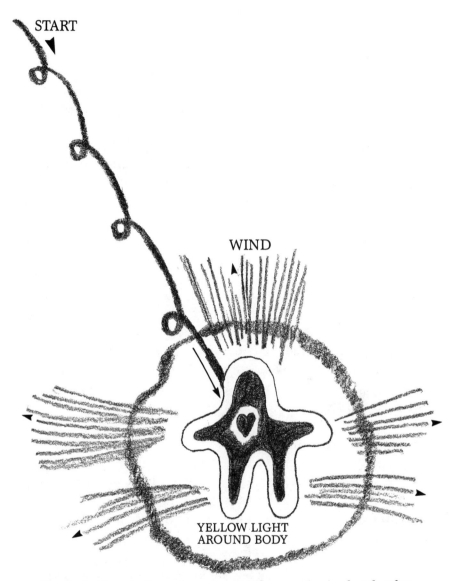

Figure 3. Cosmic Consciousness. *Sunday morning in church, after Diane had said her prayer to God, a force suddenly came spiraling down, entering her body and touching her heart. This caused a great joy within Diane, and the next thing she knew her whole body was surrounded by a golden glow of light. The joy lasted for about two hours, and then it came out of her body in the form of a wind.*

light and was able to see herself floating toward the ceiling. Then, from high up in the sky, a red line spiraled down and headed toward where she was floating.

"The line came in near my shoulder," Diane said, "and it went down to my heart. I could see my heart inside, and it was giving off a red light. But when the line touched my heart, my heart turned to a yellow glow, and red, wiggly lines started to spread out inside my body, filling it almost full."

Diane went on to say that the golden glow filled her entire body and also moved outward from her body a short distance. She then realized that her whole body was surrounded by the yellow light. At this time a feeling of great happiness swept through her.

As this child was telling me about her feelings, her voice lowered to a whisper and then stopped. This made me glance up from the drawing on my desk to the girl standing beside me. She was staring off into space with a look of angelic joy upon her face. After awhile she continued to speak, but I interrupted her and asked what had just happened that had made her stop talking.

"As I was telling you what happened in church," Diane said, "some of that nice feeling came back to me all over again!"

"Was there anything else you can remember? What are these lines here coming out from your body?" I asked, pointing at the lines in the drawing.

"Oh, that," she said, "was a wind of some sort, like air rushing out. But that came afterward."

"Where did the wind come from?"

"I don't know," Diane said, "but when I felt the happiness go through me, I started to feel a pressure of some kind inside, and it was trying to push out of me, if you know what I mean. But it couldn't get out."

"So what happened next?" I asked.

"Well, I had that happy feeling inside of me for a long time— maybe two hours. Then the wind started to come out, first from my legs. Then it came out of both hands, and then my head. After that, there wasn't any more wind rushing out. The feeling of something inside me trying to push out was also gone, and so was the happiness!"

This brought an end to the cosmic consciousness Diane experienced during her union with God, with its accompanying golden glow and feeling of ecstasy. For a child, such things may happen quite often.

A NEW SCIENCE

". . . this made sparks fly, and then there was a 'bang,' like an explosion . . ."

When Jeanne saw the red vibrations move out of her body into the air around her, she also saw one vibration cut across the path of another vibration, which made sparks fly. There was a "bang," like an explosion, but one that only Jeanne could see and hear take place. The flash of light from this explosion set off a chain reaction that ignited all the other vibrations around her body, surrounding her with a bright yellow light.

The children often referred to these vibrations, or wiggly lines, as a kind of electricity, which makes sense. What they saw in the spiritual world must be somewhat similar to the electric current produced by machines, which, traveling along wires as a form of energy, is described by scientists as a flow of electrons. The children, however, actually saw a fluid giving off light as it moved along inside a tube.

Not only did the children see a fluid, but, at times, they also saw the basic particles that made up this fluid. These particles appeared to be small, round spheres filled with a colored liquid, which seemed to be everywhere in the atmosphere—like atomic particles. When asked to describe these spheres, one girl said, "Some of them spin to the right, and some spin to the left, and some don't spin at all."

The word "atom" was first used by the Greek philosopher Democritus more than two thousand years ago. He described the atom as the smallest unit of matter; it could not be divided further without losing its identifying characteristics. This is the basis of the atomic theory, upon which modern chemistry is founded.

How was Democritus able to describe the atom so long ago, when he had no scientific equipment like the microscope to help him come to his conclusion? It is my belief that he was able to see what he called atoms, but that they were not the same atoms modern scientists refer to. What Democritus must have seen were the particles of substance that make up the spiritual world, rather than the physical particles of concern to today's scientists.

The children often talked about the "round balls," as they called them, that made up God's world. It is my belief that, like the vibrations, these colored particles are part of the basic forces that support life as we know it. It is this God force in all living things that gives them intelligence. Without this God force, living things would not exist.

Another form taken by God's power is a vibration that moves in three dimensions: the spiral. The spiral is often seen in nature: in the shape of some animal horns, in the form of many seashells, and in the branch and leaf patterns of plants. It is along such spirals that the God force moves.

Botanists have classified plants according to whether their branches and leaves are opposite from or alternate with each other on stems. Yet these branch and leaf patterns are actually based upon spirals. When the energy spiraling through a plant slows down near the tip of a branch, it moves into a circle, completing a circuit of spiritual energy. This unites the male and female spiritual forces of life, and the plant bursts forth into brightly colored flowers—a form of "ecstasy" experienced by the plant. Modern scientists have also found that plants are able to respond emotionally to different types of energies, just like people do.

After listening to the children talk about their inner worlds, and after trying to figure out the implications of their experiences, I was left with the belief that there exists a "new science" for humanity. This new science is based upon the powers of God that come from above, and yet it is probably quite similar to the laws of physics that explain energy, matter, heat, light, electricity, and so on. This new science could be termed "religious science," and the person who describes religious-type experiences in a scientific manner could be called a "religious scientist."

As an example, physical scientists have created the technology for artificially putting electricity into the human body, as with electroshock treatments for the mentally ill, but this manmade current shocks the body, even though it may help in some cases. As yet, we have not been able to duplicate the type of electricity seen in the spiritual world, which is a natural force more attuned to the physical body. When we do, we may find a cure for those who are mentally ill as well as for other sick or troubled people. In addition, scientists have been looking for some time now for extraterrestrial intelligence. It may be the religious scientists who will supply the evidence for its existence—with the help of children!

A PARTICLE OF LIGHT

The psychic children with whom I worked described many things of a scientific nature—often things of which I myself had very little understanding. Several of the children told me, for example, about experiences that seemed to indicate how a light particle is able to give off light. One boy said he saw a small, round ball (particle) in the atmosphere that had no spin to it the way many balls did. Another ball came along and struck it a glancing blow, causing the first one to spin. As it spun around, it started to circle or spiral inward, generating an increasing force or pressure until it reached the center of the spiral, where it had to stop.

"When that happened," the boy said, "the ball suddenly started spinning the other way. At the same time, it moved outward from the center of the spiral on this force of some kind that had built up. It seemed to move outward along the same path it made when it moved in toward the center."

Another boy said that when his particle moved in toward the center of the spiral there was no light shining, but when the particle reversed its motion and started to spin outward, it instantly lit up and started to give off rays of light. The light was visible as long as the particle was moving outward, but faded as the energy was used up. After the particle had stopped its outward motion, the process began all over again. In this way the light continued going on and off, over and over again.

Several children mentioned first seeing a ball of light moving within a tube and later seeing such particles of light. Figure 4 is a drawing of this made by one boy.

Figure 4. The Spiral of a Light Particle.

HOW LIGHT WAS SEEN TO TRAVEL

One eight-year-old girl said she saw clearly how light traveled. She said to me, "When I had my head down on the desk and my eyes were closed, I suddenly started to see this line of light coming toward me. It came closer and closer, and then turned around and went back where it came from. It looked like this drawing that I made." She pointed to the paper that she had handed me. (See figure 5.)

"Can you make any other drawings to show what else you saw?" I asked her.

She replied, "I can draw you a picture of how I saw little balls moving inside the light."

Figure 5. A Line of Light.

Figure 6. Spinning Balls of Light.

She went to her desk and later came back to me with a drawing (figure 6), saying, "I first saw a tiny ball start to spin. It kept spinning and spinning. Then suddenly a flash of light shot out and made a half circle. Then, after the flash of light went out, the round ball followed it, and when it came to the end of the half circle, there was another ball spinning in the opposite direction. The first ball seemed to kick the second one out and take its place. By then, the second ball had already made its own half circle of light, which curved the other way. That's how the light went, until it circled around and came back to where it started. It kept on going around and around . . . and this got me dizzy. Then everything went away."

The noted Danish physicist Niels Bohr, one of the developers of new physics, believed that light travels in two ways—as a particle and as a wave—but he did not know how this could be. The drawing in figure 6 may shed some light on how this is possible.

ELECTRICITY AND MAGNETISM

Scientists have been trying to unravel the mysteries of electricity and magnetism for years without really reaching any conclusions. They do know, however, that when an electric current flows, a magnetic field is also generated.

Some of the children in my class claimed they could see electric currents descending from high in the sky, and that magnetic forces made them wiggle (or vibrate). Even though the children made a variety of comments on this subject, what caught my attention most was their observation that a magnetic force seemed to push in the sides of the electric current as it descended. A good

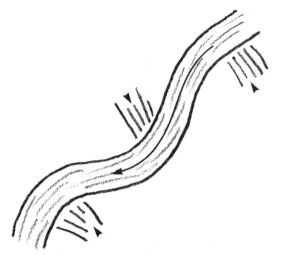

Figure 7. Electromagnetic Current.

number of the children also said that the magnetic force acted like a "wind." They could feel the wind, but usually could not see it like they were able to see the yellow electric current.

One girl did say she was able to see this wind, and that it looked like dark, streaky lines of force. She made a little drawing of what she saw (figure 7). She said, "I saw a yellow light coming down from above. It came down as a wavy line because there was a wind [a magnetic force] pushing in on the sides, first on one side, then on the other. That's how it kept on, all the way down."

According to the girl's drawing, the association between an electric current and a magnetic current may be that one is positive (and visible) while the other is negative (and not usually visible) but is felt by the children as a force of wind. If this wind force passes through the electric current and then pushes it on the other side, the magnetic force may be moving as a vibration along with the electric current, but perhaps half a wavelength behind it.

Regarding whether the wave theory or particle theory correctly explains the vibration of light, based on what the psychic children said both theories may have validity. As the girl said about her drawing, "The light I saw coming down from the sky looked like a colored energy flowing along a tube."

ANOTHER IDEA ABOUT THE ATOM

In all this research with psychic children, none of the children made drawings indicating the possible atomic action of an electron jumping from one orbit to the next and then giving off a quanta of energy. Their drawings indicated something different.

Some scientists believe that for every force there is a counterforce, and that for every particle of matter there is a particle of antimatter. The kids in school may have been able to feel antigravity and to see antimatter, but they experienced these at another level of consciousness. I would call what they experienced "spiritual force" and "spiritual matter." What the kids said they saw sounds very similar to what physical scientists describe as the atom, but the kids saw this "atom" in great detail. The following paragraphs summarize my perception of the children's experiences of the atom.

An atom is composed of a nucleus surrounded by electrons; the number of electrons depends on the type of atom. Each electron with a different-sized orbit was seen by the children as a particle of a different color. Normally, an electron stays in its orbit around the nucleus. But when an outside force strikes the atom, activating it, the atom's outer electron is hit, increasing the electron's activity into a faster spin. The electron then starts moving toward the center of the atom. It goes only as far as one orbit, at which point it moves into striking range of the next electron of a different color. This spiraling action continues inward until it approaches the center of the atom, the nucleus.

If the outside force is powerful enough, it may have enough strength to penetrate the nucleus and explode it, with a great burst of energy. If there is not enough power to do this, the spiraling comes to a halt near the center of the atom and there is a great increase in pressure within it. This starts the electrons moving in the reverse direction—outward, each in turn, along the same path on which they moved inward. At the instant of the beginning of this reverse motion, the atom suddenly lights up, giving off radiation in colors that are related to the colors of its particles and orbits. These colors may be related to the specific spectrum found by scientists for this particular atom. As the spiraling continues outward, the built-up energy is used up and the atom returns to its normal state

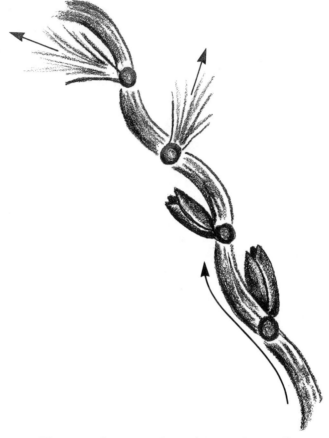

Figure 8. Quantum Growth in an Oat Stalk.

of equilibrium. Or, it could start this process over again, depending upon the situation.

THE QUANTUM THEORY AND PLANT GROWTH

In my three years of listening to the variety of things the psychic children talked about, I heard perhaps five or six of the children describe how a light vibration might move. Two of these children described exactly the same process of a light particle spiraling inward to create a great force and then exploding, with a quantity of light and energy shooting out at a tangent, after which the particle would move back onto its regular route.

Such a burst of energy shooting out at regular intervals particularly interested me, for as a science teacher with a specialty in biology I saw a correlation between this burst of energy and the growth of plants. Perhaps plant growth follows such quantum bursts of energy. This can be seen in an oat stalk, and the positions on the stalk where the seeds form. I have sketched this in figure 8.

PART II
Psychic Children and the Bible—
Is There a Connection?

PSYCHIC CHILDREN AND THE BIBLE— IS THERE A CONNECTION?

Is there a connection between psychic children and the Bible —the holy Bible that is not to be tampered with, changed, or looked at from a modern scientific viewpoint? What do things from two thousand years ago have to do with today? Why should we, in the twentieth century, be so strongly influenced by events that happened so long ago and not try to verify them, to ascertain what truth lies in them? If conditions on Earth are right for doing so, people of today may be able to tune into that other world—the spiritual world—that modern people generally know so little about.

During the Bible's time, conditions must have been right for adults to tune into God's world. They could know, and write about, what was going on in that world. That is why we value the Bible today.

As civilization advanced and conditions changed, however, people seemed to shift away from the spiritual world and move into the material world. God's world got moved into the background. But, as indicated in part I of this book, it is reasonable to suggest that young children have remained in touch with the spiritual world. They seem to have retained those special abilities that most of the adult world has forgotten: inner vision, instant knowing, and direct knowledge of the spirit. It is these special abilities—that children may always have had—that can be used to verify events described in the Bible more than two thousand years ago.

The children in my classes may have described things in the Bible that have never been described in modern times. The following sections give some insight into the Bible as seen through the eyes of these children.

THE HAND OF THE LORD WAS STRONG UPON ME

What is the meaning of the Bible verse in which Ezekiel says, "The hand of the Lord was strong upon me" (Ezek. 3:14)? Or the one in which he says, "The spirit lifted me up and took me away"? What is the meaning of Exodus 33:22, in which God, speaking to Moses, said, "I will cover thee with my hand while I pass by"?

A boy named Paul told me how one night he went out of his house and stood in the darkness. Suddenly, a large hand came out of a white cloud. It grabbed him and started to carry him off into the air. Paul became frightened about what was happening and shook himself. This made what he was seeing go away. He later drew a picture for me of what he saw. (See figure 9.)

Sometimes the children talked of seeing God in whole forms, such as a shining light or a man. Other times they spoke of seeing only a part of God, like a hand or a foot. This probably depended on the degree of altered state of consciousness they were experiencing at the time.

A person's vision of God may also depend upon the quantity of spiritual matter of which God is composed at that moment in time. This material appears to be highly compressible and highly expandable. For example, God's hand may become large enough that God says to Moses, "I will cover thee with my hand while I pass by."

One might question how God's hand could grab little Paul and lift him up. It may have been that Paul, as he shifted into a spiritual level of consciousness, was having an out-of-body experience. His spiritual body moved out of his physical body and hovered a short distance overhead. This is what he saw being lifted up by the hand and carried away. Paul, in his normal way of thinking, became frightened about what was happening. Shaking himself out of his trancelike state caused his spirit body to return to his physical body, and the experience was over.

Figure 9. "The Hand of the Lord Was Strong upon Me." (Ezek. 3:14). *A boy, Paul, went out into the night. As he stared up at the stars, he suddenly saw a white cloud, and out of the cloud came a big hand that grabbed him and started carrying him into the air. Paul became frightened and shook himself, which made what he was seeing go away.*

What has this to do with the Bible, and Ezekiel saying that the hand of the Lord was strong upon him? Ezekiel's inner state and his experience during biblical times may be unknowable. However, perhaps we can better understand Paul's modern-day experience. This boy went out into the night and looked about him. This created conditions that were favorable for him to shift into a spiritual level of consciousness very easily. Then Paul saw a large hand (such as Ezekiel's "hand of the Lord") take hold of his spiritual body and lift it into the air. However, boys of Paul's age often (but not always) resist the ways of God, so Paul did not want to be carried away. He shook himself, and this stopped his experience.

Most of the girls who described their experiences to me did not seem to resist God and God's ways, so many more of them had religious-type experiences than the boys.

THE HEAVENS WERE OPENED

According to the Bible, heaven opened up, allowing Ezekiel to see visions of God (Ezek. 1:1). The Book of Revelation of Saint John the Divine also mentions heaven opening up (Rev. 19:11). How is such a thing possible?

The children often talked about heaven during their drawing periods on Fridays, and they frequently referred to it as shining like a white light. White light is composed of the colors red, orange, yellow, green, blue, and purple—but not black or brown. One boy in class, Roger, said that he saw heaven open up and different colors descend toward him. He drew a picture of this for me, and it included the colors black and brown. I couldn't figure out why this happened, but there were many things these eight-year-old children said about God's world that I was not able to understand. Many times I just listened to what they had to say and marked it down.

Roger had gone to church on Sunday along with his parents, and he had knelt down to say a prayer. At that point he saw his spirit body leave his physical body and rise up to a place near the ceiling. Then, suddenly, he was able to see heaven. It opened up, and different colored waves of light came down and entered his spirit body up by the ceiling. This caused a feeling of great joy to fill him. Roger was so overwhelmed with this great happiness that, when his mother spoke to him about something, he was unable to answer her. It was only after he left church and returned home that he again seemed back to normal—and able to carry on a conversation with his mother. (See plate 4.)

"When I was in church on Sunday," Roger told me that Friday in school, "I saw my other body float up to the ceiling and stay there. Then, with my real body, I knelt down on the mat on top of the wood and said a prayer. Then I was able to see my body again up at the ceiling—and a good feeling went all through me.

"As I knelt there, suddenly I was able to see heaven. Then heaven somehow opened up and some kind of a black arrow, with a yellow line of light attached behind it, came down toward me and landed on top of my head. After the yellow line came down, then came a black line, followed by an orange line and a red line and a blue line and finally a brown line. Then the different colors that made up heaven appeared. First there was a red band, and next a yellow band, an orange band, and a blue band. Then a brown band appeared, and the last and the lowest band was a black one."

As the boy talked, I simply looked at his drawing and listened to what he said.

"The black arrow that first landed on my head," Roger went on, "then made an opening into my head. This allowed the colored lights to go in, one at a time, to go around my body. When they came back to the tip of the black arrow that was still in my head, each one exploded. Then my spirit body, which was still up by the ceiling, turned red. Then it was surrounded by an orange light. A yellow light appeared next around my body, and black spots were in with the yellow. Next orange lines of light came out all around me, followed by yellow lines that came out between the orange lines. All this surprised me and filled me with so much happiness," Roger said, "that I wasn't able to talk to anyone until later, when I left church!"

Some people may doubt whether this boy's story was true. But he did tell it as if he knew what he was talking about.

LIVING CREATURES
APPEARED IN A FLASH OF LIGHTNING

The Bible describes something quite different about a flash of lightning than what modern experience would predict. According to Ezekiel 1:14, living creatures were seen along with lightning. Zecharia 9:14 also describes how the power of God can manifest: "His arrow shall go forth as the lightning."

One student told me that she saw an arrow that looked like lightning moving through the air and heading toward her. Within that arrow of lightning she saw a living creature! This, of course, was what would be called "spiritual lightning." It is different from the physical lightning that we all can see.

A child, while watching a storm with lots of lightning in it, can shift into another level of consciousness within a matter of seconds. She or he can then see things and have spiritual experiences that others present may not.

"I got home from school yesterday OK," Laurie said. "But a little later when I was up in my bedroom, looking out the window at the storm, a flash of lightning came with a loud thunder and struck a tree outside. A branch from the tree fell to the ground. Then a flame of fire, in the shape of an arrow, sprang up from the branch and started coming toward me."

Laurie said that the arrow was like a rocket ship. It had flames of fire all around it, and at its end was a round ball from which smoke was shooting. As the arrow of fire came in through the window where Laurie was standing, she ducked. The fire struck the wall behind her, bounced off it, and then headed for her. It struck her in the chest, causing her body to turn white all over.

"Then," Laurie said, "like an x-ray, my heart appeared on the wall behind me. It was deep red—like in technicolor. After that, vibrations started passing through my body and I felt good all over. My body felt full of energy. This all came from God, because it happened to me before, coming from God."

Later, Laurie told me more. "Near the front of the flash of lightning," she said, "a little head of some kind of a person kept peeking out. It didn't stay long enough for me to see any more, except that something seemed alive inside and I could see the face."

Wanting to find out more about this "living creature" inside the arrow of lightning, I asked Laurie, "Is there anything else you can say about the little head that you saw?"

"No, that's about it," Laurie said. "But I do remember seeing that kind of lightning before. It first started when I was about three years old, during a lightning storm. I realized then that there was another way of life that most people don't realize."

After such a profound statement from this child who had a special gift of seeing into the spiritual world, I didn't know what to say. However, Laurie went on. "I'll draw you a picture of what the arrow of fire looked like, if you want," she offered.

"That would be nice," I said. So Laurie took paper back to her desk to draw me a picture of what she saw. (See figure 10.)

At another time I had a chance to question a different class of eight-year-old children about a recent lightning storm. About half of the class indicated having experiences that were a little bit like what Laurie had experienced. A few said that the lightning came from God. I was also surprised to hear that many of them felt happiness go through their bodies when they had their experiences.

One girl, Gail, described an experience that was somewhat similar to Laurie's. She said that during the storm a flash of lightning (perhaps spiritual lightning) struck the ground not too far away from her. The lightning then turned and headed toward her as if it had an intelligence, and knew what it was doing. At

Figure 10. "Living Creatures Appeared in a Flash of Lightning." (Ezek. 1:14). *Laurie saw a flash of lightning come at her, and near the front of it she saw a little head peeking out.*

that point she was able to see "little men" in the lightning who were moving along with it. Both the lightning and the little men entered her body—and at that instant she felt a great joy sweep through her!

What were the "living creatures" described by the Bible as appearing in a flash of lightning? After listening to many of the children, I feel that they were spiritual entities, spiritual personalities, or "little men," as Gail called them.

Perhaps the spiritual bodies of people who have previously lived on Earth go to heaven, where they exist as distinct spiritual personalities composed of particles of spiritual substance. And perhaps one way that God communicates with people on Earth (especially children) is through electricity. God may send some of the particles of spiritual personalities along electrical paths (such as lightning) so that they form small living things ("little men") who are able to influence people on Earth.

MOSES AND THE BURNING BUSH

"The bush burned with fire, and the bush was not consumed."

In the Bible, Moses encounters God in a burning bush (Exod. 3:2). How did this bush burn, and yet not burn up?

First, the fire in the bush was not the kind that people normally see. Instead, it was a spiritual fire. Therefore, the bush was not consumed by the fire in the normal way.

Before such a spiritual fire may be seen, and before such an "encounter with God" may take place, a person usually has to shift from the normal level of consciousness into another level of consciousness—the spiritual level. Conditions were ideal for this to happen to Moses at the time that it did.

Author Sholem Asch, in his book *Moses*, offers the factors that helped Moses to have this encounter with God. Moses was near a mountain that was supposed to be associated with God. He was experiencing solitude, as he was away from other people while he was caring for his flock of sheep. His experience occurred near dawn, the transition between night and day. He had just awakened from dozing, and was probably half awake and half asleep, a state of greater attunement to spiritual energies. Finally, he had been biding time, most likely thinking about what his next move in life might be—providing him with a period of meditation. All these factors together were enough for Moses to have his experience with God by means of the burning bush.

Another factor that could have helped Moses with this experience was that God told him to take off his shoes while he was standing on holy ground. Taking off his shoes created a better attunement of his body with God, as it allowed spiritual force to flow in through the bottom of his feet.

So what does Moses' experience have to do with the children in my classroom? Well, one afternoon the kids were making drawings of inner experiences that they had had recently and could still remember clearly. On this particular day, Elaine was working on a drawing that looked interesting to me as I stopped at her desk.

"What do you have there?" I asked.

"Oh, that was a burning bush I saw," Elaine said. "Last night before I went to bed, my father read to me from the Bible, the way he usually does before I go to sleep. Well, last night he read the part to me about Moses and the burning bush."

Later on Elaine seemed finished with her drawing, and I went over to her desk again. "Do you want to explain your drawing?" I asked, as we both looked down at her paper.

"This is how I saw the burning bush," Elaine said. "It was after my father had finished reading from the Bible, and he had left, that my thoughts went back into the past—to the time of Moses and the burning bush. I was about half asleep when suddenly there in front of me appeared a bush—and it was burning!"

"Was it a dream that you were having, or what?" I asked.

"No, it wasn't a dream," Elaine said. "Usually in my dreams I don't remember things very well afterward. But this was so clear to me, and I can remember everything, even now!"

"Do you want to tell me what happened?"

"Well, this is how the burning bush looked," Elaine said, pointing to her drawing. "But there was something different about this bush. It was burning and burning but it didn't burn up. When a bush is burning, after awhile the branches should burn and then fall down. But I could see the branches right through the fire, and they stayed right there.

"But there were other things that I saw, too," she went on. "The flames were reddish-yellow in color. And there were yellow balls of light around the whole bush, and these lights were circling the bush. And then as I watched, as they circled, one of the balls of light moved down into the ground under the bush and then went up the main stem of the bush—as if it had a mind of its own and knew what it was doing. Then the rest of the lights followed the same path until they were all inside the bush." (See plate 5.)

Elaine stopped talking. I was trying to think of something to say, but then Elaine started in again. "There's more to tell you. Just as all the lights had moved into the bush, suddenly there appeared the figure of a man inside the burning bush. He came out of the bush and just stood there."

"What did he look like?" I asked.

"He looked like a living person," Elaine said, "except his body was different. I could see right through him. He had long hair, and he wore a long robe. I tried to find out who he was, but he just stood there and didn't say anything. I wanted to act brave so I jumped at him, wanting to scare him away, but I seemed to go right through his body. Then he and the burning bush disappeared."

What were the factors in this child's bedtime experience that might have made it similar to the experience of the great Moses? First, Elaine was almost asleep, which would have shifted her into a spiritual level of consciousness in which she could see such things happen. Also, her thoughts were focused on the burning bush. With that special ability that children have, she seemed to go back into the past—to re-create what might have happened at the bush—although she saw herself in the picture rather than Moses.

There were several things Elaine could see, as a child with a special kind of vision, that Moses, as an adult, probably did not see. These included the lights spinning around the bush and the figure of a man in the burning bush. Moses could hear God speaking to him from the burning bush, but he could not see God. As an adult, he may not have been entirely "pure of heart," and thus was not able to see God even though he could hear God speak. The child, still "pure of heart," could actually see God. As the Bible says, "The pure of heart shall see God"!

Elaine saw balls of light circling the bush that acted as if they knew what they were doing. Then a spirit person appeared. In the spirit world, a person can travel through space as an intelligent flow of energy and then later convert back into the form of a spirit being. The size of the spirit being depends upon the amount of energy involved. The balls of light that Elaine saw were most likely the energy form of the spirit being she later saw.

Elaine, seeing the spirit person come out of the bush, did not know that she could pass right through spiritual substance. So she was surprised that, when she jumped, she went right through the person. At that point, in switching her experience to thinking with her rational mind, she may have realized that the person she was seeing was not physically tangible. When this happened, the whole scene disappeared!

This incident with the burning bush illustrates the power of thought under the right conditions. The mind acts somewhat like a magnet in that it can pull past events in history out of the "collective unconscious," as Carl Jung called it. Elaine did this, and the burning bush appeared before her. Later, when she jumped right through the man standing in front of her, her mind released its magnetic hold on the scene before her, which then disappeared.

FOR GOD IS LOVE

Children often describe a variety of feelings they experience as coming from God. Love is one such feeling that they talk about. But how can a person describe the feeling of love to someone else? It may be difficult.

When I had my own encounter with God, as described in part IV, a kind of love filled my body at one point. When this feeling of love flowed through my body, it packed a powerful wallop. A man was standing in from of me at the time, and suddenly I had a feeling of great love for him. Perhaps "compassion" would be a better word—but at the time the only term that I could think of for my feeling was "heavenly love."

If we had ESP, or psychic abilities, as most children probably have, we could look inside our physical bodies and see what is going on in our spiritual bodies. We could, for example, see our hearts. When the children talked about seeing their hearts, they were seeing not their physical hearts but their spiritual hearts, which exist in the same location in the body.

Many people do not understand the full function of the heart. Those in the medical field know well how the mechanical heart works but are unaware of the workings of the spiritual heart. Every healthy spiritual heart, within its particular physical body, has vibrations of a particular wavelength that are in harmony with the rest of the body. That body itself also gives off specific vibrations, which might be called its aura.

As physicians have discovered in their attempts to transplant the heart, when a living heart is taken from one body and placed in that of another person, there is usually trouble. The physical vibrations of the recipient may not be in harmony with those of the transplanted heart, so the body tries to defend itself against these "foreign" vibrations and rejects the new heart.

I believe that each physical heart has a particular spiritual heart that grows up and develops with it. This spiritual heart is the center of the emotions that the person experiences, including love, joy, peace, fear, anger, and all the other emotions that make up the individual's personality.

The Bible, which is more spiritual than physical in its meaning, often mentions the heart and its various feelings: "My heart is glad" (Ps. 16:9); "Sorrow hath filled my heart" (John 16:6); "Thou hast put gladness in my heart" (Ps. 4:7); and so on.

The medical profession does not recognize this other dimension of life within the fleshly body that can affect a person's health. Doctors may refer to the spiritual dimension as "just the imagination," and its effects as psychosomatic—not "real" trouble. However, its effects can be very real trouble!

What can psychic children tell us about this spiritual heart? One day in class, a boy named Duane had something he wanted to say about it and how the feeling of "love" came to him. Duane talked to me about a great happiness that he felt within him, which he said came from God. He made a drawing to show what had happened to him. (See figure 11.)

As we both looked at his drawing, Duane said, "It looked like electricity. I saw it come wiggling down, and as it got close to me it divided into two lines. At the same time I could see my heart, and it was giving off red rays, the way it usually does. When the current divided into two parts, one line came in and hooked on to one of the red rays on one side of my heart, and the other line hooked on to a red ray on the other side of my heart. Just as that happened, my heart suddenly started to glow with a bright, yellow light! This made a feeling of great happiness—and love—inside of me!"

Duane did not know it, but he had given a pretty good explanation of how it is possible to feel God's love in the heart.

As Duane and I talked some more about his experience, he mentioned several more times that the rays coming from his heart were "pure red." I heard this idea of the heart being "pure red" from the children at other times, as well.

The child, I feel, is born with a spiritual heart that is pure, and not born in sin, as some people would have us believe. It is the adult heart that may not be pure red in color, having picked up various sins, or impurities, in normal life. It would be sort of a "murky" red, or an offbeat color. "To be born again" could mean to cleanse the spiritual heart of such impurities—and so have the pure red heart of a child again. The "confession of sins" is supposed to be one way to purify the heart.

Duane's drawing shows how some people may experience God's love, or what might be called "spiritual love." If this kind of love is experienced frequently by certain people, they may not have the urge, or need, for physical love. This spiritual love may far exceed in intensity the physical love experienced by most people on Earth.

However, most adults on Earth cannot feel God's force within, and so male and female hearts seek each other out. If their hearts

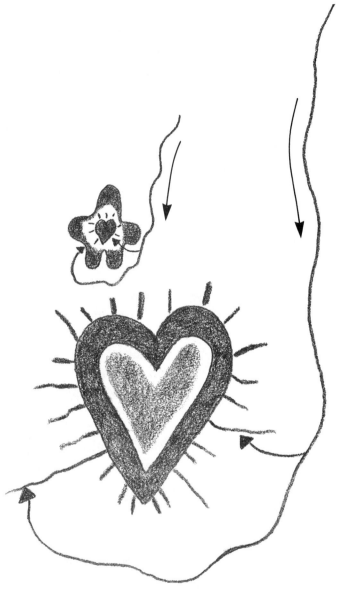

Figure 11. "For God Is Love." (1 John 4:8). *One day Duane was thinking of God when suddenly he was able to see an electric current come down from the sky, divide in two, and then make contact with his heart. At that instant his heart started glowing with a yellow light, and then a feeling of a great love from God flowed through his body.*

start to glow (which neither can see), a great happiness is felt within. They "fall in love."

Another day in school, Duane told something else that had happened to him. There was a girl sitting across the room who caught his eye. As their eyes met, Duane said that he was able to see a force come out of the girl's eyes, head in his direction, and then enter through his eyes and go down into his body. Shortly after that he felt an excitement start up within him. Then he was able to see vibrations start to come out from his heart. This was the same thing that happened when the force of God came down to activate his heart.

Some people seem to think that modern civilization is obsessed with sex. However, it may be that the sexual force and the God force are one and the same thing!

As is portrayed in Duane's drawing, the God force can move down from above and go into a person's heart. Duane's story indicates that the God force descends like electricity and, moving as a wave, is also electromagnetic in nature. It carries the two electrical charges—positive and negative—which could also be called the male and female forces.

When a child receives the God force, which contains both the positive and negative charges, the child feels complete. This creates a feeling of spiritual love, or God's love, within the child's body. However, as the child grows up and gets to be about twelve or thirteen years old, a change takes place in the child's physical body. Starting at about that time in life, only one charge of electricity descending from above enters each human body. The male body receives the positive charge, while the female receives the negative charge. These electrical forces then activate each human body into either manhood or womanhood.

As a young person matures, there is an urge to complete his or her spiritual life, because each young man and young woman has only half of God's force inside his or her body. So, like a magnetic force, the opposite sexes are attracted to each other. A spiritual love develops, which results in physical love between the two of them. Physical union brings together the positive and negative currents of God, which creates great happiness within.

THAT CHRIST MAY DWELL IN YOUR HEARTS

The Bible tells us that Jesus may dwell in our hearts (Eph. 3:17). How is this possible? It is not that Jesus actually lives in our hearts, but that he, as a spiritual being, may come down from above and move into the human body for a few moments.

A spiritual personality, such as Jesus, may exist in a variety of sizes—depending perhaps on how much spiritual substance (or spiritual energy) that personality is composed of at a given point in time. Spiritual substance seems to be highly compressible, so a man-size Jesus might be reduced to a much smaller entity who can fit inside a physical human body, especially within the heart.

The heart is the center of many actions associated with the spirit body. A child who is gifted with the special ability of being able to "look within" can see what is going on in the heart.

One day in class, the children were talking about what heaven looked like. A girl named Bonny mentioned that she saw Jesus in her heart. This started a lively discussion about the idea of Jesus being in the heart. Bonny then told a story about what had happened to her in church on Sunday, just after she had finished saying a prayer.

"I saw heaven too," Bonny said. "Then, a little later, a bright, yellow light started coming down from there. When the light was about halfway down to Earth, it got so bright I had to shut my eyes and turn away. But the light still kept coming down toward me. It came into my body through the top of my head and then went down into my heart—where it stopped. I felt a great happiness go through me, and I could see that Jesus was there, in my heart. I saw him, and I talked with him. A little later Jesus said that he had to go back up to heaven."

Bonny then said that Jesus left her body and moved back up toward heaven along the same path of light that he came down on. She drew a picture of what she saw. (See figure 12.)

What does Bonny's experience in church have to do with other teachings in the Bible, besides the teaching that Jesus may be able to enter the heart? Well, what happened to Bonny may be a little similar to what happened to Paul when he was on the road to Damascus.

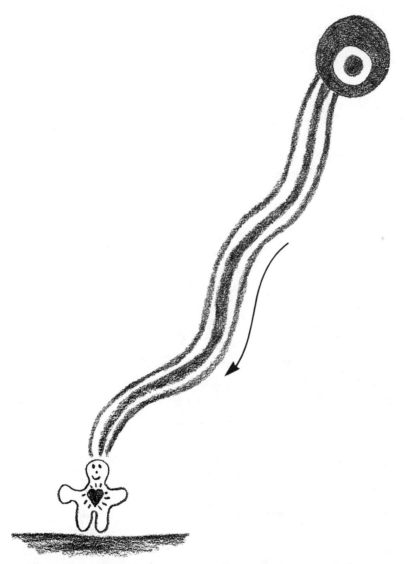

Figure 12. "That Christ May Dwell in Your Hearts." (Eph. 3:17).
Bonny saw a bright, yellow light come down from heaven and enter her body. Then it went into her heart, where it stopped. As it did so, a great joy filled her body, and she saw that it was Jesus who was in her heart.

For Bonny, the light from heaven was so bright that she had to turn away so as not to hurt her eyes. Paul (or Saul, as he was called before his conversion) probably did not turn away when he saw the light coming down at him—and so was blinded for three days. This light from above, as seen from a spiritual level of consciousness, must be very intense. A child usually can take more of this type of spiritual light than a grown person, but even Bonny had to turn away from it, as it was hurting her eyes.

When Paul was making his journey to Damascus, he probably didn't know what hit him when the light came at him. He could have been worn out from the trip, tired, thirsty, and perhaps traveling in a dazed state. There were enough conditions present for him to have shifted into another level of consciousness. In this altered state, the light came to Paul and was seen by him. However, he didn't know enough to stop looking at the light. Whether Jesus went into the spiritual heart of Paul, we do not know, but Paul did say that Jesus talked to him, so we at least know that he was there.

A VOICE CAME OUT OF THE CLOUD

In the Bible there are a number of stories about voices speaking to people. In most of these stories it is God who is speaking. For example, in Mark 9:7 a voice came out of a cloud, and it was God's voice. But how can a voice come out of a cloud?

During one creative expression period, Marian told me that she had heard a voice coming out of a cloud high in the sky, and she felt it was God who was calling her. Of course, this was probably not the regular type of cloud that one normally sees in the sky; instead, it was most likely a spiritual cloud, made up of spiritual substance and energy. One can see such a formation when one has moved to another level of consciousness or when one is, as it says in the Bible, "in the spirit." It is then that one may also be able to hear a voice coming from a cloud.

Marian said she not only heard the voice, but that she also heard it as it went through her body. And she could see the letters that made up the words as well! This ability to see words from God may have been described in the Bible. John 1:1 says, "In the beginning was the Word, and the Word was with God, and the Word was God."

Marian's experience began one night when she was at home in bed, about half asleep. It is during such times that children seem to shift into a spiritual phase of consciousness, in which they see many things.

"When I was lying there," Marian said, "I started to see things happening high up in the sky. First I saw heaven. Then there were clouds, and some were of different colors. Then I heard a voice calling my name, saying, 'Hello, Marian. . . . Hello, Marian.' The sound came out of two clouds. One cloud was red, and the other cloud was green."

"How can a voice come from clouds?" I asked.

"I don't know, but I saw it and I heard it," Marian said. "Shall I make a drawing of what I saw?" I said yes, and Marian took some paper and started to draw. (See figure 13.)

Later on, she used her drawing to explain that the sound was carried along on the red and green vibrations that came from the red and green clouds. The two vibrations descended side by side, entering her body through the top of her head. They then circled her body as the voice kept calling, "Hello, Marian. . . . Hello, Marian." After returning to her head again, the two vibrations left and went back to where they had come from.

Marian said she could see the vibrations going through her. She could also hear the sound of the voice inside her body and could actually see the letters of the words that she heard. "The voice," she said, "was first soft and then loud, then soft and then loud again, and that's how it kept going." She also said that the soft part of the voice had a low, deep tone and was made by the green vibration, while the loud sound had a high tone and was made by the red vibration. "And I'm quite sure," she added, "that it was God who was calling my name!"

Another girl at a different time also said she had heard a voice calling her in the night and felt it was God. She also heard the voice as first soft, then loud, then soft again, and then loud again. She said that this depended on which part of the vibration a word was positioned, and she drew me a sketch of how this looked. If

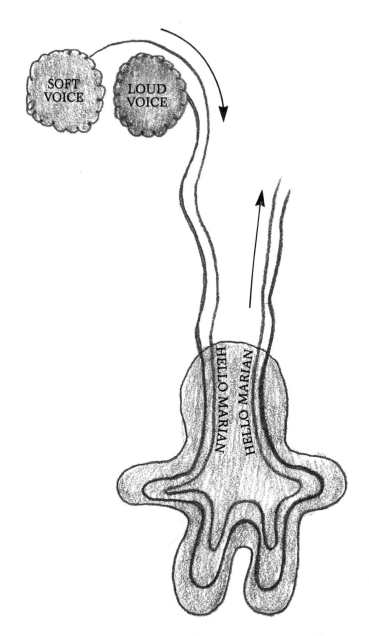

Figure 13. "A Voice Came out of the Cloud." (Mark 9:7). *Marian, an eight-year-old girl in school, thought she heard God calling her name over and over again. She looked up and saw the voice coming from two clouds high in the sky.*

I had questioned Marian in more detail, she might have been able to give me the same information, and her sketch might have been like the one in figure 14.

After listening to many children and realizing that they may have a special ability adults do not have with respect to the spiritual world, I stopped doubting whether the things the children told me were true or not. I simply acted as a recorder for the events that happened to them.

Throughout the history of life on Earth, many people have told stories about hearing voices, or about their names being called by voices, or about being told by voices to do various things. Sometimes these have been good voices, and good things have happened to the listener. Other times these have been bad voices, and bad things have happened.

In the Old Testament, the third chapter of 1 Samuel describes how when Samuel was a young boy he heard a voice calling his name three different times on the same night. The old prophet Eli, who was nearby, told him that it was God who was calling and that Samuel should answer God. This Samuel did, and the voice from above stopped calling. (It is thought that Samuel was about eight years old when he heard God calling him.)

Of course, when voices come and the listener is not "in the spirit," then the person is not sure that the voices even happened. A scientist could hear voices and term them a "flash of inspiration," possibly leading to some new discovery. Someone else might call the voices a "hunch." Another might say, "I had a feeling I just heard something!" And so on.

However, according to *The Magic Power of Your Mind* by Walter Germain, there have been others throughout history who have heard the voices clearly. The late Dr. George Washington Carver said that he often heard God speaking to him.

Figure 14. A Voice Calling in the Night.

Thomas Edison heard voices that guided him in his work, for he knew nothing about electricity when he first began working with it. He said, "If I had not worked under the direction of a Supreme Intelligence, my work would never have been done at all."

Socrates heard a voice that guided him most of his life. Whenever he was considering certain acts that were not good, the voice would tell him not to do them. At times he didn't listen to the voice and he got himself into trouble. However, this was a voice that seemed to come from within him, rather than from above.

Joan of Arc started hearing voices when she was twelve years old. This started one day at about noon when a bright light, brighter than the sun, appeared in the sky. A voice came down from the sky, directing her to do certain things. Her experience was recorded and has been made a part of history.

Mary Baker Eddy, the founder of Christian Science, was a young girl when she heard a voice from above calling her name. She felt it was God, but she would not respond to the calling. This went on for almost a year. Finally she was advised to answer the voice. She did so, and it stopped.

THE KINGDOM OF GOD IS WITHIN US

The Bible tells us that, according to Jesus, the "kingdom of God is within [us]" (Luke 17:21). How can God, and God's kingdom, come down from above and enter a human body on Earth? As I mentioned previously, the substances that make up the spiritual world are highly compressible, and only small amounts of the substances that make up God and the kingdom of heaven may descend from above to enter a human body that is spiritually attuned. When this happens, the person may see, using "inner vision," God, Jesus, angels, and so on.

Laurie, a girl in class, told me a story that suggests that the kingdom of God may be seen within the body. While she lay in bed half asleep after saying her evening prayers the night before, she began to see her chest glow with a white light.

"Then," Laurie said, "angels, many of them, came down from

heaven. And with them came God. Jesus was there, too. They came into my body, here." Laurie pointed to her chest area.

I asked if they were in her heart.

"No, I don't think so," she said. "They seemed to be a little below my heart. But they made a great happiness inside my body. The angels were singing, and they made such wonderful music inside of me!"

Later Laurie explained that, at first, she saw God only as a bright yellow light descending from heaven on a huge wavy line. As she remembered it, there were also two lines that seemed to hold in the bright shining light as it moved. The word "heaven" also appeared and descended along with the light. She saw the word and heard it spoken as it moved toward her. Then her name, Laurie, appeared on her forehead, and she was surprised to hear it spoken. At that point she realized that God was speaking to her.

Another girl, Marian, also claimed to see God and the kingdom of heaven come down from above—but this happened to her at breakfast time. Her mother had put her breakfast on the table, but it was a warm June morning and Marian just sat there not eating the food, in sort of a dreamy state. Suddenly she saw a light start descending from the sky above her, spinning as it moved. The light approached her and then stopped spinning in front of her. Out of it came a small figure of a man, which quickly expanded into a full-sized person. He had long hair and wore a purple robe.

"I knew that this must be God," Marian said, "because a nice feeling came over me, which I've felt before. Then suddenly, from a picture of Jesus on the kitchen wall, small lights appeared and started whirling about. Then Jesus seemed to come to life, and he floated down and stood on the floor next to God. Finally I said to them out loud, 'Hi!'

"My mother gave me a look from where she was standing in the kitchen. She said in a loud voice, 'Who are you talking to?' I didn't answer her. Then I said again, 'Hi!' and they answered back, 'Hi!'

"My mother looked around again, and in a louder voice she said, 'Who are you talking to?'

"I said, 'I'm talking to God.'

" 'Eat your breakfast and stop imagining things!' she said, and there was an angry tone to her voice.

"I didn't know what to say to my mother, but finally I asked God, 'Should I eat my breakfast?' And he answered, 'Yes, do as your mother says and eat your breakfast.' I don't believe that my mother heard God talking, but I did. She came over to where I was sitting, and I could tell by her look that she was getting madder.

" 'That's enough of that!' she said. 'Now eat your breakfast!' So I ate my breakfast. God and Jesus talked to each other for awhile. I couldn't understand what they were saying because it sounded like some other language. Maybe it was Latin—I don't know. Then they left. I finished my breakfast and then came to school."

About a week later Marian had another experience with the kingdom of God, but unlike Laurie, her experience was outside her body. Marian was in bed, still awake but getting drowsy. She saw a cloud come down and hover over her. It was made of gold and silver sparkling balls from which God, Jesus, Mary, and many angels emerged and filled her room. A feeling of great joy swept through her. She got out of bed and went to tell her mother, who was asleep in another bedroom.

As Marian walked slowly in the dark to her mother's room, God and all the others followed. Marian woke up her mother.

"What are you doing—walking around in your sleep?" her mother asked.

"Mommy," Marian said, "God is here, and Jesus, and Mary!"

"What . . . again?" her mother said. "Go on back to bed and let me sleep."

So Marian went back to her bed and went to sleep.

Can anything in Marian's story be verified by something written in the past about a similar experience? Marian's experience of looking at a picture of Jesus on the wall and then seeing Jesus coming to life has been described before. It happened to Saint Francis of Assisi. In her book *Mysticism*, Evelyn Underhill describes how a painted picture of Jesus on the wall suddenly seemed to come to life, and from the lips of Jesus, Saint Francis heard his name being called. The two of them spoke awhile, and Jesus gave Saint Francis instructions about what to do with his life. Then Jesus vanished. He also appeared to Saint Teresa of Avila as a living person who revealed to her some of the secrets of life.

I realized, in listening to many children reveal secrets about life largely unknown to the modern adult world, that the whirling action mentioned by Marian was a key factor in the unfolding of their experiences. This whirling enabled Jesus to appear to Marian. At first she saw small balls of light, and then she saw the balls of light go into a spin. This spinning action was mentioned by many of the children, and it seemed to initiate the appearance of spiritual individuals from heaven.

It seems that if conditions are right and a child shifts into a spiritual level of consciousness, then the thoughts in the mind of the child at that time are powerful enough to materialize a being from above. This spiritual being then appears to the child in much the same way that a physical person would appear.

THE STAR OF BETHLEHEM

When Jesus was born in Bethlehem, a star appeared in the East. According to Matthew 2:9, Herod then sent three wise men to see if the omen of Jesus' birth was true. Alternatively, according to Luke 2:8, it was three shepherds who made the journey. The truth of the situation is hard to determine today. However, every year about Christmastime there are many articles in newspapers and magazines by astronomers or other scientists attempting to determine the nature of the star that was seen over Bethlehem. Such stories are, to me, really a lot of nonsense. After listening to many gifted children describe what might have happened, the closest thing I can determine is that seeing the star must have been a spiritual experience.

If the so-called "star" suddenly appeared in the sky, guided the three wise men or shepherds to Bethlehem, where Jesus was supposed to have been, and then stopped in the sky right above Jesus' birthplace, this "star" must have been a spiritual ball of light that had intelligence and knew what it was doing. Probably only those who were at the spiritual level of consciousness at that time would have been able to see it.

Adults, most of whom have lost the ability to "be in the spirit," do not understand very much about God's world and how things function there. But the children often mentioned seeing "balls of light" in the sky that moved and acted as if they knew what they were doing or had intelligence.

In listening to the children, I also found out that God and other heavenly beings who can be seen only in spirit can also change into spiritual forces or energies that can move about, sometimes rapidly and sometimes slowly, in the sky. Usually, anybody who happens to be in the right altered state of consciousness at the time that this is occurring can see these spiritual energies moving about.

One day I had the children project themselves back into the past to about the time of the birth of Jesus to see what they could come up with. Several children mentioned the star that was supposed to have been in the sky at the time. They indicated that it was not a real star but a round ball of light that guided the way for people below to follow. A few of the children drew pictures of what they saw.

Gail also glimpsed a scene along a road at night. She said, "I saw three shepherds moving along this road at night when the star, shining very brightly, suddenly appeared above them. It frightened the three men. I heard one say, 'I'm afraid!' Another asked, 'What shall we do?'"

Then the star (which was actually a ball of light) opened up and Gail saw a ray of light move down toward the men. Out of this ray of light an angel appeared. The angel talked to the shepherds and told them not to be afraid—that she would lead them.

"Then," Gail said, "everything faded away, and I couldn't see anything more."

No one knows for sure what really happened so many years ago. I do feel, however, that it must have involved a spiritual encounter rather than an actual star, as the astronomers would have us believe.

MY HEART IS GLAD

A number of places in the Bible refer to a person's heart as containing such feelings as joy, sorrow, and gladness (Ps. 16:9, for example). Perhaps it might seem that this is not actually true — that this is just a figure of speech and that such feelings cannot really be in the heart. However, since the Bible is mostly spiritual in nature, the feelings it refers to would most likely be those within the spiritual heart rather than the physical heart, even though both are located in the same area.

Children can offer much understanding about the spiritual heart, which seems to be the control center of the spiritual being as well as the center for various emotions. One of these emotions is the great joy or happiness that many of the children felt within their bodies.

A boy at another school told his teacher that he was able to express his feelings in color. For instance, he said, to feel happy he would see the colors yellow, orange, red, and dark green all together. The teacher was pleased to hear this, but she didn't understand what he meant and so she didn't follow up on his experience any further.

When I passed this information on to my class, Marian immediately responded. "I'll show you a drawing," she said, "of those same colors. They also make a happy feeling inside of me. I see them every night, and they make my heart glow!"

Marian brought the drawing up to my desk later and explained what it was about. (See plate 6.) "I was having some nice thoughts about something up in heaven when suddenly I got a response. High up in the sky I saw this light coming down. It was round like a ball, and it had the colors green, red, orange, and yellow in it. As it got nearer to me this ball of light kept getting smaller and smaller. It got so small that it was able to pass into my body through the top of my head. It started moving around my body as a wiggly line, giving off sparks as it went. The sparks marked the path the ball took as it moved along inside of me. When the light came to my heart it stopped, and all the sparks that were around inside of me moved into my heart, too. When this happened my heart seemed to swell up, giving off a red glow of light until my whole body seemed lit up. Then I felt a happiness spread out all over inside of me!

"Pretty soon," she continued, another ball of light came from someplace, but it seemed like it was a bad thought that was trying to get into my mind. It was a pinkish-colored light. This light and the other ball of light both seemed to know what they were doing except that the pinkish light wasn't quite so smart. It came in through the top of my head, too, and started to cause a bad feeling inside of me. It appeared to be looking for the trail that the good light made, which had already disappeared inside my body when all the sparks had moved into my heart. So the pink ball didn't know where to go. It then backed up on the trail it had made and left my body. Where it went after that I don't know. Anyway, the happiness that was inside of me stayed with me for a long time."

This was what one girl had to say about having good feelings inside her body—and they came from her heart.

JESUS CASTS OUT UNCLEAN SPIRITS

The Bible tells a story about a man who was tormented by unclean spirits (Mark 5:13). He asked Jesus to help him, and Jesus commanded the unclean spirits to come out of the man's body, which they did, going ir.to the bodies of a flock of sheep that was close by. This drove the sheep mad, and they rushed over a cliff, fell into the sea, and were drowned.

Who were these unclean spirits? Other names for them might be "bad spirits" or evil spirits" or even "devil spirits."

What were they like? Phineas P. Quimby, a pioneer in the study of psychic experiences and a healer, claimed to have seen such evil spirits. According to his life story as told in *Health and the Inner Life* by Horatio Dresser, Mr. Quimby was the man who healed Mary Baker Eddy, the founder of Christian Science, at the time she was seriously ill.

Quimby seemed able to chase unclean spirits out of sick people. Somehow he could see these little "imps," as he called them, as they left a sick person's body and often tried to get into his own body. An ordinary person would not have been able to see this, but Quimby, being "in the spirit" at these times, could see what was going on. He described these imps as being various sizes, ranging from six inches to two feet, with each one having a separate identity. They would buzz about him like a swarm of bees, trying to get into his body. But Quimby knew that by concentrating his thoughts on God he had the power to repel evil spirits, and soon he would see them flying off like the wind. He also believed that the evil spirits were created by a sick person's negative thoughts.

Emanuel Swedenborg says in his writings that good spirits and bad spirits are both under the control of God. Good spirits build up while bad spirits tear down. In the overall pattern of life, this dualism is necessary and makes life on Earth function. If everything born on Earth were to live and nothing were to die, there soon would be no place for new living things on the planet.

The concept of dual spirits was also expressed in the book *The Dead Sea Scrolls* by Millar Burrows. The section entitled "Manual of Discipline" discusses the fact that there are two spirits in people, which exist as outside forces as well: the spirit of light and the spirit of darkness. Like Swedenborg, Burrows claims that both are creatures of the one God and are regulated by God. Some people may call these their "guiding spirits." While adults cannot usually see good or bad spirits, children, who can easily look into this so-called invisible world, can often see them.

One day in school a girl came up to my desk and surprised me with a little sketch she had made. She then told me that she could look inside her body and see a bad spirit living on one side of her body and a good spirit living on the other side. (See figure 15.)

If spirits do live inside the human body, this might help explain some things about life that so far have not been explained very well. As mentioned previously, Socrates, the famous Greek philosopher, heard a small voice inside himself most of his life that told him what to do. The advice given him by this voice was very good, and if he didn't follow it, he often found himself in trouble. In *Mysticism*, Evelyn Underhill gives examples of other famous people in the past such as Saint Francis and Saint Teresa who heard a good voice within—and then went on to make history.

Human beings have risen above a method of living upon which

all other life on Earth depends: instinct. Humans have become free of this locked-in force, and instead possess free will—the ability to choose. We can choose between good and bad, and in doing so we can destroy ourselves by choosing evil or rise toward God by choosing good. This may be due to the quality of dualism that is found within every human being.

A reference to this was made in A.E. Waite's book *The Holy Kabbalah*, a mystical book on the secret origins of much of Jewish tradition. This book states that a person, when first born, has two spirits within: one on the right side of the body and the other on the left. The spirit on one side is like that of an animal, while the spirit on the other side is like that of a holy person's mind.

Books on religion often state that angels and devils are part of the spiritual world that is outside a person's body. Swedenborg wrote a great deal about good and bad spirits. In particular, he made the following points:

1. In every person there are spirits from hell and angels from heaven.
2. For anything to exist there must be an equilibrium. There is a perpetual equilibrium between heaven and hell. A spiritual sphere of good life—or bad life—flows forth from every individual.
3. It should be known that the hells are continually assaulting heaven and endeavoring to destroy it . . . but that the Lord continually protects the heavens.
4. God rules both heaven and hell, keeping an equilibrium between the two and thus allowing humans to be free and to choose which way they want to go.

These are only a few of the ideas espoused by Swedenborg. It should be remembered that the hells are continually assaulting human beings on Earth, trying to knock us down. But when we need to be protected from such forces, we can direct our thoughts or words to God above. This usually causes the bad forces to disintegrate.

One day in school, an angel came down from heaven to help a boy, Andy, out with his troubles. On that particular morning, while everyone else was working, Andy just sat at his desk staring

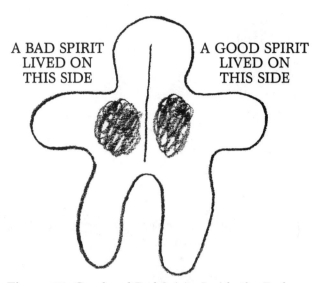

A BAD SPIRIT LIVED ON THIS SIDE A GOOD SPIRIT LIVED ON THIS SIDE

Figure 15. Good and Bad Spirits Inside the Body.

off into space with a troubled look upon his face. A few minutes later, as I watched him, I saw his distress vanish and a happy look come over him. A little later Andy started in on his schoolwork and was soon working like the rest of the class.

My curiosity was aroused about what had happened to Andy to cause this change, and I called him up to my desk, where we could talk quietly and privately about what had taken place. Andy said, "I was being annoyed by these 'little men' who often cause me trouble. I saw an opening in the ground where the little men came from . . . and they had what looked like pitchforks in their hands. They climbed up inside my leg, crawled up my body, still on the inside, and then came out and stood on my hand that was there on the desk.

"Then they jumped up and went in through the openings in my nose," Andy went on. "Then they got up into my mind. They all got around in a circle and then they all started annoying me with their words. They were telling me to do things I didn't want to do. 'Don't go to school tomorrow,' they said. 'But I want to go to school!' I said. 'Then don't do good work in school.' 'But I want to do good work in school!'

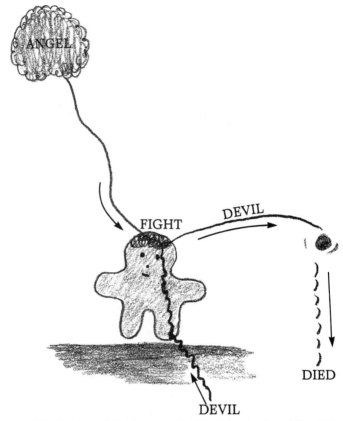

Figure 16. An Angel Defeats an Evil Spirit. *Andy, while sitting at his desk, was troubled by an evil spirit that got into his mind and was annoying him. Andy called on an angel from above for help, and the angel came. There was a fight, and the bad spirit was kicked out. Andy then felt happy inside and went back to doing his classwork.*

"And so it kept on," Andy continued. "I looked up to heaven to see where the angels were who usually help me out when I'm in trouble. But they probably didn't see these bad men come out of the ground. I saw one angel fly out from heaven and head for Earth. Then for some reason she turned around and went back.

"The little men kept sending bad thoughts to my mind. I was looking around for help when a ball of light came down from above and other little men jumped out. These were good little men. They came in through the top of my head, and started right in to fight the bad men.

Figure 17. The Good Spirit. *Vera saw an angel (or good spirit) come down from a fluffy, white cloud high up in the sky.*

"The fighting seemed to give me a stomachache because right at that same time I started to hurt there. Pretty soon the good men won and chased the bad ones away. The stomachache stopped, and then I felt happy again inside!"

Andy also said that the day before he had had similar trouble with one devil that had gotten into his mind and was annoying him. But an angel came down quickly from heaven, battled with the devil, and kicked him out. Andy then felt good inside and was able to get back to his schoolwork in a hurry. He made a drawing to show what he saw take place. (See figure 16.)

I also heard many other children talk about the causes of the good and bad feelings within their bodies. Vera, a girl in class, described her experiences a few days later. She saw a good spirit (an angel) cause a very nice feeling within her and a bad spirit (a devil) cause a bad feeling. Vera said that the angel came down from a fluffy white cloud up in the sky. The devil came from below; he was a little man with green skin and black whiskers, wearing a blue shirt and red pants. He also had a three-pronged black fork with which he jabbed her to cause the bad feelings. (See figure 17 and plate 7.)

The Bible says that Jesus chased unclean spirits out of people. It is difficult to know if those unclean spirits were the same kind of bad spirits that the children in school talked about, but they sound quite similar. The children's experiences may therefore help clarify the accounts mentioned in the Bible that occurred almost two thousand years ago.

SEEING ANGELS
"There were angels all over."

Angels are mentioned many times in the Bible as being in heaven. They can also come to Earth as so-called "messengers of God" to talk to people, to help and guide people, and to carry out various acts for people on Earth. In addition, there are people who think that some of these intelligent beings who assist us are people from outer space who come into our solar system by way of so-called "flying saucers." Whether or not this is true, I do know that plenty of communication is occurring between the spiritual world and Earth.

One can recognize spirit beings or angels if one's body becomes attuned to the spiritual world. This can happen under such various conditions as great stress, illness, prayer, or being half asleep.

The children had much to say about angels and other such spiritual beings. One girl, Doreen, was able to see an angel very clearly. She saw a ring of light over the angel's head and understood how it worked. She even had a conversation with her.

One day during the noon hour at school, I was eating a sandwich and relaxing when Doreen poked her head past the classroom door and asked if there was anything she could do—clean the boards, pass out paper, and so on. She probably just really wanted to talk; many of the kids who stayed at school for the lunch hour liked to come in and talk.

While Doreen was asking if she could help, she kept moving into the room, evidently with the idea of staying there. So I let her stay. She was a shy girl during classtime and usually didn't talk much then, but at other times she had plenty to say.

On my desk was a book, *The Littlest Angel*, about a movie the class was going to see in a few days. Doreen saw the book and immediately started talking about angels.

I felt quite sure that many of the children, at one time or another, saw angels, as did people in the Bible and other great people of the past who had guiding spirits come to them and lead them to better ways of life. So I asked Doreen, "Have you actually seen an angel yourself?"

Doreen thought for awhile and then said, "Yes, I did see an angel once, and it's still very clear in my mind."

"What happened?"

"I was lying in bed, half asleep but thinking about angels, when I saw one. The angel came down from the sky and stopped near me."

"How did she look?" I asked. "Did she speak or say anything?"

"She didn't say anything. She just touched me on the shoulder, and when she did that I suddenly felt good all over. She was dressed in a white gown. She had white wings and her hair was yellow. There were sparks—white sparks—spread out into the air from her gown, and there was a yellow ring over her head."

"What did the ring look like?"

"It looked like a shadow, but it was clear enough to see. There were yellow sparks shooting out as the ring spun around."

"What do you mean the ring spun around?" The idea of the halo over the angel's head spinning around was new to me, and I became quite anxious to hear more about it.

"Yes," Doreen said, "the ring spun around. First it spun around to the right once, then it spun around to the left once, then to the right, then to the left, and that's the way it kept up."

"Did you see anything else?" I asked.

"When the angel came down from the sky I thought she would use her wings, but she didn't. She just seemed to float straight down toward me."

And that was about all Doreen had to say about the angel. However, according to my notebooks, about two years later I again heard the story about the halo over an angel's head spinning around, and in such detail that it left me quite astonished! Jennifer, another eight-year-old girl, had made a drawing at home. She came in one noon hour to talk to me about it. (See figure 18.)

Jennifer put her drawing on my desk, and we both looked at it in silence for awhile. Then she said, "This is an angel who I see. She seems to be near me all the time and always on my right side or on my right shoulder. She speaks to me, and I'm the only one who can hear her. I can see her mouth move when she is talking, but no sounds come out."

"Where does the sound come from?" I asked.

"The sound comes out of the ring of light that is always above her head. When she doesn't talk, the ring stays still. When she whispers, the ring starts to spin around. When she talks out loud, the ring seems to get thicker as it spins around, and it gives off sparks—like electricity."

Jennifer stopped talking for a moment and then continued. "The sound comes from the two round balls that are on opposite sides of the ring." She pointed to them in her drawing. "They are both reddish yellow in color. When the angel speaks, one of the round balls shakes. This makes the sound of the words that the angel speaks. Then the small tube in the center of the large ring wiggles. When it does this, it seems to open up at a seam, and a liquid that is thick spreads out a short distance."

"What's this liquid like?" I asked. I didn't know anything at all about the subject of halos over angels' heads, but I didn't want to appear ignorant (which I was) about what she was telling me.

"The liquid," Jennifer said, "looks like the Crisco my mother uses at home when it's hot and flowing down the can. When it comes out of the seam, the ring brightens up, and rays of light come out—both outside and inside the tube."

I was in somewhat of a daze as I sat there at my desk looking at the drawing. This child was telling me about the inner structure of a ring of light over an angel's head. Most adults, if you pinned them down for a definite comment, would probably classify angels under the heading of "fairy tales" and let the subject go at that.

"The Crisco-like stuff is colored as it flows along inside the tube," Jennifer continued. "All the colors are mixed in together. The small tube looks like plastic that bends easily. It is clear, and

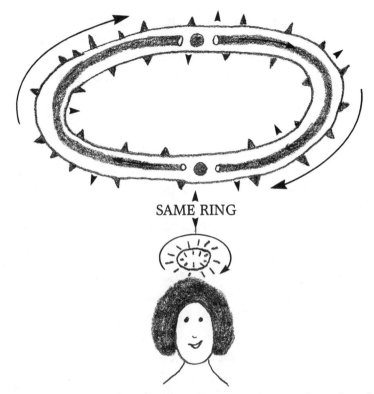

SAME RING

Figure 18. The Angel's Halo. *An angel spoke to Jennifer, and as she did so, a ring of light over her head spun around.*

you can see the colors inside moving along. When there is a sound, you can see the tube wiggle around to the other side until it strikes the round ball of light that is there. Then you hear the next word the angel speaks.

"But the second ball doesn't wiggle. It sends out a bluish-yellow line of light around the other half of the ring. That is how it keeps going as long as the angel speaks. The sparks that move out from the ring are yellow. The big ring that makes the halo looks like plastic or glass, because I can look right through it and see what is going on inside.

"That's about all I can tell you," Jennifer said, "except that the angel appears without a body. Just her head is there and the ring of light. There are wings, too, but they don't seem to be attached anyplace, and they stay right there as if that is where they belong."

The next day I talked some more with Jennifer about the ring of light over the angel's head, and I learned something else. She said, "Only half of the ring glows at one time. The angel talks so fast that the ring looks as if the whole thing is shining at the same time, but I remember that this is not so. When a wiggle goes around one half of the ring, it suddenly stops just before it gets to the other side, and it does not hit the other ball as I said before. On either side of these two balls of light there seems to be a wall that keeps the wiggles apart. When one half of the ring shines, the other half does not.

"And that," Jennifer concluded, "is how the light over an angel's head works."

GOD IN HEAVEN

"Jesus had rounded cheeks and looked younger,
while God had thin cheeks and looked much older."

The name "God" has been bandied about so much in recent years, and in such an irresponsible manner, that there may be some doubt as to whether God really exists. However, Jeanne described both how she saw God and how she talked with God. She saw him as a man, or as "our father who art in heaven."

Moses and other Jewish prophets of the Old Testament spoke to God but did not see God; their dialogues were between heaven and Earth. Jeanne was able to leave the Earth and visit with God above in her spiritual body. Swedenborg also describes how he visited God above and then returned to write about it in his books.

Who is this God "who art in heaven?" No one knows the answer for certain. Perhaps God was some saintly person who once lived on Earth before the time of recorded history. Jeanne said in her encounter with God that he looked very old. Or God might have been a human being with godlike qualities who came from someplace in outer space. Then again, God may have evolved spiritually, as our civilization developed, created from the many gods and goddesses of primitive people and so becoming the "one God" that the Hebrews proclaimed.

Mystics of the past have also expressed the concept of a "God beyond God," or a "God who created heaven and Earth" in the beginning. Swedenborg said that he was able to see another God — a shining ball of intelligent light, high up in the sky above the heavens, which was seven times brighter than the physical sun. It is this God (as sun) that penetrates all living things on Earth to give them intelligence to live by, an intelligence perhaps known on Earth by the term *instinct*.

If we are looking for order within the entire universe, and not just within our own solar system, then we have to assume that God (as a spiritual sphere of intelligent light) must also be in communication with the gods of all the other life centers throughout the universe. Therefore, we could assume that there is a supreme God over everything, perhaps a "God of the Universe." Where this force came from in the first place I wouldn't even try to guess.

With respect to our own heaven and Earth, human beings may be the only ones on this planet to have developed a high level of reasoning power—enough to move us away from the instinctive forces of God the sun and toward the forces of God in heaven. In listening to God's words, people on Earth have been able to change their ways of life. This has been manifested through the development of civilization and through the societies and organizations that people have created, especially the religions of the world. It is because of the churches and synagogues we attend that we do not forget God in heaven, perhaps whom we knew as children.

As the Hebrew mystics tell us in the Dead Sea Scrolls, there is hope for humanity to develop itself and become in harmony with the forces from above—even for all human beings to become like the "holy ones" on Earth who are in direct contact with God. Furthermore, it may be the children who are the "holy ones," the ones who have the ability to know and be with God.

PART III
Classroom Discussions

BRAINSTORMING IN THE CLASSROOM

The method I used in my classroom to turn ordinary third-grade kids into psychic kids included the technique of brainstorming. This technique involved throwing questions out to the class and then seeing what kinds of answers the children came up with.

Brainstorming is also used in programs with "gifted children" throughout the United States. Some of these programs may be good, others may not be. As one leading educator involved with a program for the gifted recently commented, there are a lot of awful programs in existence across the country. I don't know whether this educator is right, but I do feel that if educators would try the brainstorming technique and other ideas expressed in this book, they would develop truly good programs for the gifted.

In my own program, I used brainstorming only at the start. Later on it wasn't necessary, as the children developed their own latent abilities to come up with novel ideas about life.

In the years following my research, when I checked with several authorities on programs for gifted children in the United States about my program, none of them showed any interest in it. They had their own work to promote and didn't want any of my "far-out" ideas. Therefore, I have presented my approach in this book. The chapters that follow contain conversations and discussions with the students that show how my method developed in the classroom throughout the years of my teaching.

Using my method, all third-grade children could become psychic children (or "gifted" children). The gift that this approach helps to develop far surpasses most abilities that the adult world generally utilizes. Possibly, at this time, children really are in many ways superior to the adults living on Earth.

FEELING THE VIBRATIONS
October 10

After a morning's recess period of vigorous outdoor play, the children came into the classroom perspiring. I had them put their heads down, close their eyes, and breathe deeply several times, using a *method* (comment 1) I had described before. This helped them relax their bodies and cool off quickly. I also told them to watch for anything *going on inside their bodies* (comment 2) that we could talk about that afternoon during the creative expression period.

After the rest period was over, hands started waving. It seemed that the children didn't want to wait until afternoon to express themselves—they wanted to talk now! Laurie waved her hand vigorously. When I called on her, she said, "I stopped being tired within a few seconds."

Larry said, "I felt something creep down my arm. And it was wiggling!"

Rita said, "I felt something crawl *up* my arm."

I thought that the wiggling was supposed to go *down* the arm. It would bear watching to see if others expressed the idea of the wiggling going *up* their arms.

That afternoon, I explained to the class that the wiggly lines they were feeling inside their bodies might be *vibrations* (comment 3) of some kind, although I didn't know what kind they were. I then told the class to try and see or feel these vibrations inside themselves. "This time," I said, "don't stop watching them right away. Keep looking. Follow the vibrations and see where they go. Trace them back, if you can, and see where they come from."

The children tried again, putting their heads down. They were silent for about *fifteen seconds* (comment 4), and then one head came up with a hand waving. Then another hand came up. Then hands were waving all over.

"I felt it! I felt it!" someone exclaimed. I didn't know who had gotten so excited because voices buzzed all over the room as the children started telling each other what had happened. After calming the class down, I was able to hear what they had to say.

Pete announced, "I felt the vibration crawl down my hand, and it stopped in my fingers!"

Kathy said, "I felt it go down my legs, and it went into my toes!"

Helen commented, "I felt like going to sleep."

Mary said, "Mine went up into my head!"

With each response, I became more excited myself. The children were laughing, and I was laughing.

Laurie raised her hand and, in an excited voice, said, "I felt the vibrations spread all over my body! This made me feel *happy! And peaceful* (comment 5) all over!"

I was laughing so much at this point that it was hard for me to stop. What Laurie had just described was the very same thing that had happened once to me, and it had also caused a great joy to flow through my body.

The sound of laughter had almost come to an end when Scott stood up, very excited, and said, "I followed a vibration down my hand and out my fingers, and then . . . pop! . . . and then there was a flash of light!"

After saying this, Scott broke out into loud laughter. The whole class started in again, and so did I. I laughed so hard that tears flowed down my cheeks, and I had to wipe them away with my handkerchief. Some of the children were looking at me—a little amazed, perhaps, that a teacher would be so uninhibited.

Meanwhile, the class was still buzzing with excitement. There was about five minutes left in the creative expression period, and I wanted to talk to Scott about his "popping" noise. After quickly passing out paper, I told the children to draw whatever they had seen when their heads had been down.

While the class quickly settled into making drawings, I went to Scott's desk and asked him to tell me more about the explosion. He said, "I saw the vibration move down into my fingers. It felt like *electricity* (comment 6). When it got to the tip of one of my fingers, it seemed to get stuck (comment 7) and couldn't get out of the finger. Finally there seemed to be enough power of some kind that the vibration suddenly shot out from the tip of my finger and into the air. When it did this, there was a flash of light and the popping noise!"

Comments Made at a Later Time

1. *The method.* By accident, I happened on this method of having the children rest their heads on their desks, close their eyes, breathe deeply, and then concentrate on something. Later, when I studied the methods used by the mystics of the Far East, I realized that this method was somewhat similar to the ones they used in their searches into the secrets of life. The mystics led lives of solitude in caves, used special deep-breathing exercises to adjust their inner bodies for attunement, and meditated on what they were searching for. When the children closed their eyes, they were in solitude; when they breathed deeply, they were using one of the breathing practices of the mystics; and when they concentrated on something, this was the same as meditation.

2. *Going inside the body.* Looking into the body may also be called "inner vision." There is information on this process in promotional literature of the Rosicrucians. The great people who belonged to this order, such as Benjamin Franklin, Isaac Newton, and Francis Bacon, were supposed to have the power of "inner vision." I believe that all children have this power, but that in the normal process of growing up, it is lost.

3. *Vibrations.* A Tibetan mystic of the past claimed that the key to the riddle of creation is in the hidden power of vibrations—which most people on Earth do not even know exist. The children described a great deal about these vibrations—how they moved, where they came from, what was in them, and so on.

4. *Fifteen seconds.* The method I used was such that the children could shift quickly from the ordinary world into the "invisible world" that the average adult never sees. To the child this other world is not invisible, for he or she can see what is going on in it very clearly.

5. *Happy and peaceful.* These are two words I heard many times from the children to describe how they felt when they were attuned with their inner bodies and became "one with the

universe." This peace and happiness is not the kind that a person would experience in normal life, but is a deeper and more beautiful feeling than most people ever imagine. Happiness as experienced by these children was most likely very close to the ecstasy experienced by mystics and prophets of the past—it seems to be a celestial type of happiness. Rabbi Joshua Loth Liebman, in his book *Peace of Mind*, made a reference to this peacefulness when he chided the reader, "You would have peace but would not look within."

6. *Electricity.* This was a common word used by the children to describe the activity inside themselves. Scott's description sounded like electrical activity: he felt the electricity move down his arm, get stuck, build up pressure, and then finally pop out into the air, making a noise and giving off a flash of light.

7. *"It seemed to get stuck."* The low intensity of the current flowing through the children's bodies might have created difficulty in moving the energy through parts of their physical bodies. It would therefore become blocked at, for example, a joint of a finger. If there was enough buildup of force at the blockage point, then the electrical current could surge across and continue on its way. If all such currents were able to leave the child's body at about the same time, a feeling of great peace or joy would fill him or her.

FEELING PEACE WITHIN THE BODY
November 7

The children had worked for a long period of time on their language papers, and I could see that their little hands were getting tired. Several had put their pencils down to rest their hands awhile. One boy was shaking his hand to get the tiredness out. A girl clenched her fist and then relaxed it, trying to get rid of the tired feeling.

This caused me to remember a comment made by Laurie several weeks before. When the vibrations were spreading throughout her body, she said that she suddenly felt a great happiness inside her—along with a peaceful feeling.

Laurie's description brought back memories of a similar feeling that had come over me in college—a feeling of peace inside my body—achieved through a technique motivated by the simple act of writing. I discovered the process by accident while taking an exam at college. I had become so tense and nervous about this exam that I could not write at all. However, by alternately *tensing and relaxing* (comment 1) the muscles in my writing arm, I willfully, *with my thoughts* (comment 2), tried to push the tensed area down the inside of my arm.

At that point I was very surprised to feel something moving down my arm and then stopping at my wrist. After trying again, I felt that "something" move down into my fingers and then out into the air. At that instant, a great feeling of peace swept through me, and at the same time my body *felt attuned* (comment 3) and in harmony with the whole universe. This was an awesome feeling! I felt ready to start the exam, although it was at least fifteen minutes after the rest of the class had started. However, I wrote so swiftly, and the answers came to my mind so quickly, that I was the first one to finish and walk out of the classroom. This was the only time in my life that this happened to me. Therefore, I wasn't sure if the children in my class were experiencing the same thing that I had.

The period after language class was the creative expression period. I immediately explained to the class how it might be possible to remove the tiredness from their arms by tensing and relaxing the muscles of their arms and letting the tired feeling drain out; I mentioned nothing about the possibility of a peaceful feeling. Then I had the children try this to see what would happen. They put their heads down, closed their eyes, breathed deeply, and dangled their writing arms down along the sides of their desks. They squeezed their fists, and then let go, then squeezed, then let go, and so on.

Quite soon, perhaps in fifteen seconds, I could tell that some changes were taking place. The children were starting to stir about after the quietness, and hands were waving.

Helen said, "I felt a vibration go down my arm, but it stopped at my wrist." She pointed to where it stopped.

"Try some more," I said, "and see if you can move it down and out your fingertips."

Scott waved his hand excitedly as if he wanted to speak in a

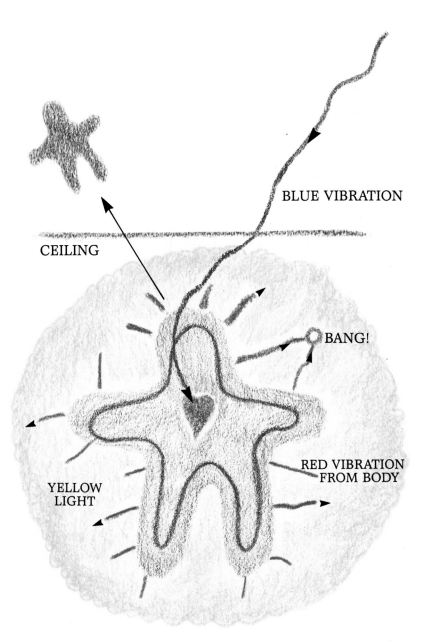

BLUE VIBRATION

CEILING

BANG!

RED VIBRATION FROM BODY

YELLOW LIGHT

Plate 1. An Out-of-Body Experience. *One night while she was in bed, Jeanne said her evening prayers. Later on, when she was half asleep, she saw events take place that sent her spirit body floating toward the ceiling of the room. She looked back and saw her other body still in bed. Then Jeanne wandered to different places, including heaven, where she talked with God!*

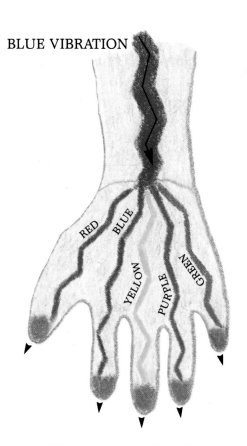

Plate 2. The Healing Hand.

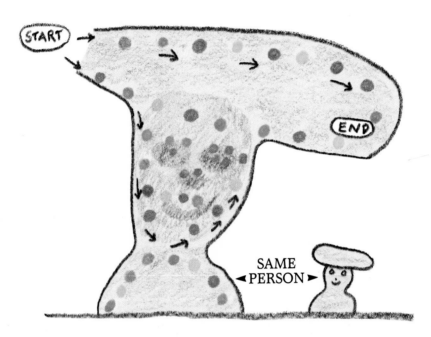

Plate 3. A Friend Materialized. *Children have spiritual friends they talk to whom no one else can see. One girl saw her friend take shape right in front of her out of colored particles.*

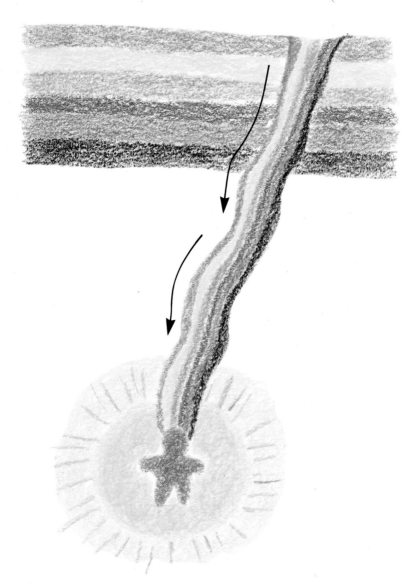

Plate 4. "The Heavens Were Opened." (Ezek. 1:1). *One Sunday morning Roger was in church with his parents. He knelt down to pray and, as he did so, he saw heaven open up. A light descended, entered his body, and filled him with joy.*

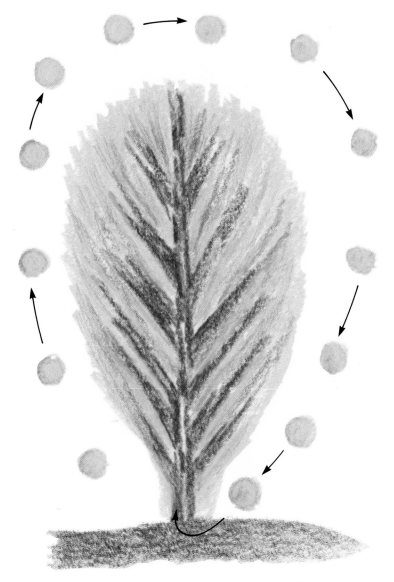

Plate 5. Moses and the Burning Bush. (Exod. 3:2). *Elaine saw a bush that was burning, but its branches did not burn and fall down.*

SAME BALL OF LIGHT

Plate 6. "My Heart Is Glad." (Ps. 16:9). *Marian saw a ball of light come down from high up in the sky. It entered her body and caused her to experience a feeling of great happiness.*

Plate 7. The Bad Spirit. *Vera saw a devil (or bad spirit) come up from the ground below.*

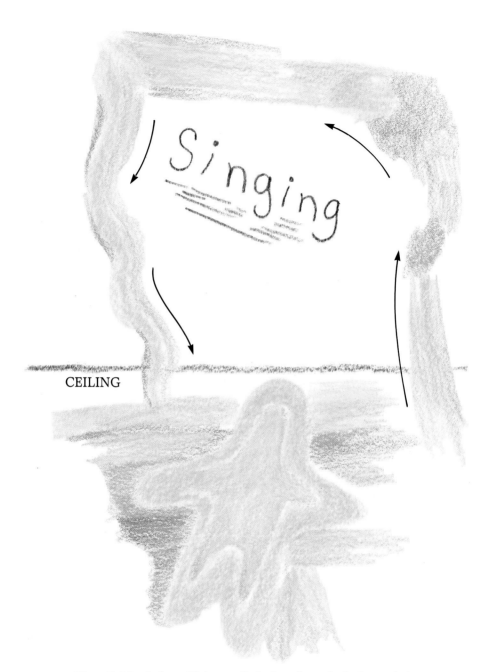

Plate 8. Music from Heaven. *Cathy heard angels singing up in heaven. There was a flash of light, and sounds came down in lights of different colors. Cathy heard music around her body, and also inside her body. Later the sounds went back up into the sky.*

hurry. "I felt something move down to my hand," he said, "and then it jumped across!" He pointed to a knuckle, indicating how the vibration had jumped from one bone to the next and over the joint. "And," he went on, "at the same time I saw a flash of light." The class always became excited whenever Scott had something to say, so they started laughing.

Debby said, "How is it that everybody feels something and I feel nothing?"

Then Laurie waved her hand again. "I felt the vibration move down some more, but it stopped at one of the finger joints."

"You keep trying some more and see if you can get it all the way out," I said and went back to listening to other comments. Then Laurie again waved her hand.

"I did it! I did it!" she exclaimed. "It went out through my fingertips and into the air. And when it did that, I suddenly had a wonderful feeling all over my body! It was a peaceful feeling inside of me!"

This last statement from Laurie was what I had been looking for. She experienced the same feeling that had overwhelmed me. In both cases, this occurred when the vibration left our bodies to pass out into the surrounding air. At that point, a sudden feeling of great harmony or peace filled us.

I asked the whole class, "How many more of you had that nice feeling?" About ten hands went up out of a class of thirty. I don't know if they all felt the same thing, but there were enough hands for me to realize that this technique could work to create peace and harmony within the body, as it had once done for me. In my own experience, this feeling was such that I had seemed in tune with the whole universe. It was such an incredible feeling, and most people on Earth may not even know that it exists!

Comments Made at a Later Time

1. *Tensing and relaxing.* The technique of first increasing pressure in various areas of the body and then relaxing the same areas is a big help in restoring the spiritual body to its full force inside the physical body. Deep breathing works the same way, increasing the pressure within the lungs on inhalation and then removing the pressure on exhalation.

2. *" . . . with my thoughts . . . "* Thoughts in the mind generate a force, or flow of energy, within the body. One time I sent a thought from the outer surface of my left cheek toward the inside of my body. An instant later, I saw a yellowish vibration of about four waves move along the path of my thought.

3. *Felt attuned.* When the spirit body becomes one, or in harmony, with the physical body, then it is attuned.

FALLING ASLEEP

April 14

After the rest period, several children said they wanted to talk about things they had seen when their heads were down on their desks. Later in the day, when they were finished with their regular classwork, they got paper from me and drew what they had seen.

Bruce said that when he had his head down he fell asleep for a moment and then woke up. Figure 19 is his drawing of what he experienced. It was quite similar to what others had drawn in the past. It depicted the spinning action that makes people dizzy while they are falling asleep. However, Bruce explained his drawing in more detail than anybody else had.

"At first there was a tiny yellow ball of light. It was spinning around in one spot. Then it started to move away, and it made a circle of yellow light. But it wasn't a real circle—after it went around once, the yellow light ended up a little distance away from where it had started. After this one circle had been made, the yellow light suddenly changed to an orange light. This went around once also and ended up even further away from the center. This spinning around kept up, and the colors shifted to red, then to green, blue, purple, brown, and the last one was black."

Bruce took another breath of air and continued. "As the black line finished its circle, it moved in toward the middle as if it knew what it was doing. It went directly to the yellow center and banged into it. This caused a big explosion! Then black smoke covered everything and I must have fallen asleep, because I don't remember anything else until I woke up a little later."

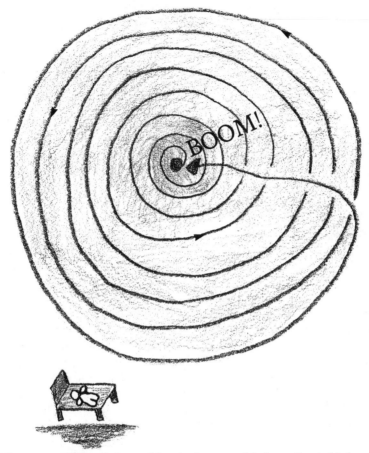

Figure 19. Falling Asleep. *A boy in class saw this formation in his head just before he fell asleep for a few moments. It spun around and made him dizzy. As the black line made its final spin, it hit the yellow center with a bang. This caused an explosion, at which point the boy fell asleep.*

Comments Made at a Later Time

The drawing by Bruce was one of the many drawings made by the children that left me amazed! Physical scientists have been trying to figure out what happens to people when they fall asleep, but so far they haven't been able to figure out much even though they have written a lot about it. Perhaps the spiritual scientists of the future may get the closest to what really happens, for falling asleep may actually be a psychic action.

The spiral Bruce saw inside his head may be a form of motion common to many activities in life. Several children in class described the action of the "atom" in almost the same way. In his book *Cosmic Superimposition*, Wilhelm Reich, whom I would call a spiritual scientist, wrote about similar movements of the psychic forces, which he called "orgone" energy. Many ancient drawings also portray a similar spiral action.

Mystics of the past talked about spiritual action and the eightfold stages of life, which may be connected to the eight colored spirals in Bruce's drawing. A book called *The Mystic Spiral*, by Jill Purce, is filled with illustrations depicting activity similar to that in Bruce's drawing. This book is subtitled *Journey of the Soul*. Perhaps Bruce's drawing shows how after the explosion, when a person passes from the conscious to the unconscious realms (or moves from the awake stage to the sleep stage), the force of the explosion moves the spirit body out of the physical body, and the spirit body (or soul) goes on a journey (or the person has a dream).

Not only do the mystics describe this spiral action, but so do some of the famous artists of the world. These artists may have retained some of the abilities they had as children, and this shows up in their world-famous art. Pablo Picasso, Vincent van Gogh, Marc Chagall, and others all painted spiral or wavy colored lines flying through space or performing other activities.

It may be that, in sleep, the spirit body leaves the physical body and goes to distant places (as in a "dream"). Or the spirit body may stay close by, but outside the physical body, and become recharged during the night. By morning, when the two bodies are reunited again, the physical body is refreshed and ready to start on another day of life upon the Earth.

FEELING THE POWER OF GOD
December 12

I had put words on the blackboard from our reading book, a story about Christmas. After the reading was over, I erased most of the words but left a few, such as Bible, angel, and heaven, to be used in the creative expression period. I asked the class what they knew about the words I had left on the board. In response to the word *Bible*, they said:

"A big book."

"A story about Jesus."

"A book of old stories."

Then someone mentioned the word "God," and a girl asked, "Who is God?"

"Yes," I repeated, "Who is God?" A sudden silence came over the class for awhile.

One child finally said, "God is a man."

Another commented, "My mother said that he is always standing right there in front of you. But I don't know why I never bump into him."

"I don't understand it," another said. "My mother said that Joseph was the father of Jesus, and then she said that God was the father of Jesus. I really don't know who is his father."

These were all the comments from the class at this time. The question asked by one of the children—"Who is God?"—could have led into a discussion that had been building up in my mind for several weeks, but I wasn't sure how to proceed with it.

Later, during the creative expression period, I talked a little about my feelings about God in a general sort of way. Then I said, "Another day we'll see if we can know God better, but not today."

When the children heard that I wasn't going to say anything more about God, they expressed disappointment. They wanted me to go on. So, as this was the Christmas season and the air was filled with stories about *Jesus, Joseph, and Mary* (comment 1) and good spiritual feelings (and although I was of the Jewish religion), I decided to continue with the discussion.

My mind searched for ideas about how to proceed. Finally, I asked the class, "When you pray, you bow down your head to speak to God. But do you find God down below or up—as in heaven?"

"Up!" the class let me know.

"Right," I said. "When you speak to God, look up. And you can talk to God, too. Just say what you have to—as if you were talking to anybody. Tell God what you want. If you want God to come down so that you can feel God inside you, say so. You might say, "Dear God, come down from heaven and come into my body." The children giggled. I had to grin myself at such an explanation.

"You could also lift up your arms as you are looking toward

heaven and speaking to God (I lifted up my arms to show them), and your arms could be like the antenna on a radio or television set. If you are alone, in a church or your home, you could say the words out loud, but here in class just say the words to yourself. God will hear you and *may* answer you by sending down a force that you might feel inside your body." (This same thing had happened to me once when I was a soldier and in an army chapel—a force came down from the sky and filled my body. See part V.)

"After you have spoken to God," I went on, "be still a little while and you might feel something come into your fingers, then go down your arms and into your body."

By this time the whole class had *their faces lifted upward* (comment 2) and their arms up like antennas, but their eyes were open and they were giggling. So I had them close their eyes, be quiet, and speak to God in their thoughts.

I watched their faces. This was a crucial moment. I didn't know whether they would feel anything, but I wanted to find out if the power of God could really come to many people, as I believed it could, or only to a selected few.

As I continued to watch the children's faces, I noticed, after about ten seconds, that their expressions had begun to change. Something was going on! In about another ten seconds, hands started waving in various parts of the room as the children tried to get my attention. I didn't call on anyone at this point, so the children started talking to anybody who was nearby. A buzz of excitement filled the room.

The first one I called on was Maureen. She was giggling and seemed quite excited. She said, "I felt something come down and go into my hand, but I don't know what it was!"

Roberta said, "I felt something move down my arm!"

Pam remarked, "Something went into my body. And something 'funny' is going on inside of me!" A puzzled look was on her face.

Debby commented, in a somewhat discouraged tone, "Why is it I never feel anything?"

Others were feeling things. Some started to feel warm inside. Then Laurie waved her hand with excitement. She said, "I felt it! I felt it go down into my body—even down into my toes! Then it went *up and down in my body three times* [comment 3]! And I'm very warm all over inside!" Others also reported feeling heat.

A suggestion to these children was almost like a direct order, since most of them did whatever they were told—even if it was only a mild suggestion. Also, most of them could see or feel whatever was going through their minds. Therefore, there were key points of information that I did not suggest to or share with the children, as I wanted to see if they would have certain experiences spontaneously, rather than at my suggestion.

For example, I did not suggest to the children that they might feel heat in their bodies, although I knew this was a possibility. I also did not suggest to them that they might feel something go down into their toes, and yet Laurie described this experience exactly. The up-and-down sensation that Laurie experienced, however, I had never heard of before.

By this time, children were talking all over the room. This was certainly a creative expression period, because it seemed that every child felt something and wanted to share it with someone else, all at the same time. It seemed also that I had stepped into a situation that was more than I had bargained for. So, with difficulty, I quieted down the class and had them start a writing assignment that was due the next day.

Laurie, however, was having difficulty starting the assignment. I went over to her desk and asked her, quietly, what was the matter.

"I'm still getting warmer and warmer inside my body," she said. "It feels like there is *a fire burning inside of me* [comment 4]!"

I had Laurie go and stand by a window where cool air was coming in. In a few minutes she went back to her seat to do her work.

I made a mental note to myself never again to have an entire class of eight-year-old children try to feel God's power all at the same time. The force was too powerful. Such children are probably able to feel God easily enough, without any outside help!

Comments Made at a Later Time

1. *Jesus, Joseph, and Mary.* To me, the life of Jesus was part of the life of the Jewish people and of the Jewish religion.

2. *".. . their faces lifted upward ..."* Saint Francis of Assisi, a person who contacted God many times, used this method. One night he was seen kneeling and praying to God with his face and hands raised upward toward heaven. A light was seen coming down from the sky and landing on top of his head. Out of the light a voice spoke. Later, when Saint Francis was asked about the light, he said that God had been in the light and had spoken to him.

3. *".. . up and down in my body three times ..."* The number three occurs quite frequently in reports about spiritual activity.

4. *".. . a fire burning inside of me ..."* Most people would not understand the concept of a fire burning inside the body. This is a spiritual fire, and it has been experienced and written about by several people. Lama Govinda, in *Foundations of Tibetan Mysticism*, says that the heat produced in a process he refers to as the "yoga of the inner fire" moves up and down the body. His description of "ascending and descending movements of the inner fire" sounds very similar to Laurie's experience.

ELECTRICITY IN THE BODY
January 27

In our science lesson we read about electricity—how it exists in batteries, how it moves through wires, and so on. Then one girl spoke up and said, "Sometimes I see electricity going through my body."

This started a discussion on electricity in the body. I told the class how it might be possible for people to have such vibrations inside their bodies. Then I suggested that they experiment with this by bringing a finger from one hand close to a finger on the other hand and seeing what happens. They could also bring a finger close to the finger of someone else sitting close by.

Within a few minutes, Bonny became quite excited about what happened to her. "As I put my two fingers together," she said, "I felt the electricity flow down one arm, go through the two fingers, and then move up my other arm and into my chest. It kept going around and around, and I felt my body getting warmer and warmer. Then, just as it got so hot that I was going to stop it by taking my fingers apart, I suddenly saw my body light up—all over!"

Another girl, Ann, put out her finger and brought it close to the finger of a boy sitting nearby. Suddenly she saw a flash of light jump from her finger to the boy's, and her finger started to feel very warm. Then, as she watched, both of their fingertips started to glow with a pink light! (See figure 20.)

Elaine saw an electric current come down from the sky in a wave formation. The electricity, which she said acted like lightning, struck the ground, bounced along for awhile, and then went back up into the sky again.

"When the electricity came down from the sky," she said, "it left a glowing trail behind it. After it hit the Earth, the glow disappeared and only the outline of the current remained. It looked like two lines side by side, moving along the ground, like a road. Then when the electricity headed back up to the sky again, along the same path it came down on, the glowing light started again."

Of course, the electricity that the children saw was not what we normally think of as electricity, but it was this type of energy viewed from a psychic perspective. Later on I asked the class, "Where does the electricity come from?" One child said that it came from heaven. Another said that it came from a large shining ball like the sun. Another said that it came from God.

When two boys tried touching hands, the electricity that flowed between their hands clashed, or made a barrier, and did not pass into each other's hands. When two girls touched each other's hands they had the same reaction, although several girls said that the current did pass through.

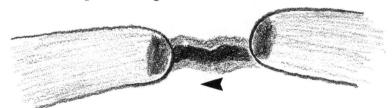

Figure 20. Electricity in the Body. *When Ann brought her finger close to the finger of a boy sitting nearby, she saw a flash of light jump from her finger to the boy's, and her finger started to feel very warm. Then, as she watched, both of their fingertips started to glow with a pink light.*

Donna touched Mark's hand for a short time. Then she said, "When we touched hands and I closed my eyes, I saw electricity come down from the sky, enter my head, go around inside my body, and then move into my heart. Then these wiggly lines came out from my heart that made me feel very nice all over!"

Donna became excited as she went on, "Then the electricity went out from my hand and into Mark's hand. I was able to see inside his body, too. The electricity went around his body and then into his heart, and the same kind of wiggly lines came out of his heart that made the nice feeling in me. Then Mark looked at me, and gave me a nice smile! But an odd thing happened. My hand seemed glued to Mark's hand as if a magnet was holding them together!"

Comments Made at a Later Time

Physical scientists know practically nothing about the electricity in the human body described by the children. However, according to Claude Bristol in *The Magic of Believing*, one scientist, Professor H.S. Burr from Yale University, after many years of research put together some equipment that could detect a current in the human body. He found that an electric current of 1.15 millivolts flowed from a person's positive right hand to his or her negative left hand.

When Burr recorded the electrical charge from an injured finger, he found that the flow of electric current in the body was reversed, with a negative charge being emitted from the hand that was previously positive. Also, the flow of current was almost ten times greater than in uninjured hands.

The ability of electricity in the human body to change its direction of flow may be an important key to understanding how the body works and is able to heal itself. I once read about a formerly institutionalized mental patient who said he had felt a change within himself similar to a shifting of the flow of a current to the opposite direction. "That," he said, "was the start of my recovery—to good health!"

PEACEFULNESS AND THE "LITTLE MEN"
February 5

I had left the word "peacefulness" on the blackboard, where it had been placed during a reading assignment. Later that afternoon, in a discussion period, I asked the class of thirty kids to describe how a peaceful feeling occurs inside the body. They put their heads down on their desks to try to find out.

Later, seven children said they saw lines or waves come down from the sky and enter their bodies, causing peaceful feelings. Four saw vibrations spread out from their hearts to create this nice feeling. One saw the peacefulness form from something that looked like a wheel. Bruce felt strong rays spread out from his body and then go out to other people. Mary felt peaceful when she saw the word "peace" and heard it being spoken inside her body.

Bonny had a longer story to tell. She said, "I saw a bright yellow light come down from the sky and go into my body. On this line of light, which seemed to stay where it came from in the sky, I saw letters come down—and they made the word 'God.' Then God came down on that same path of light and went into my body. He wore a bluish-purple robe and had brown sandals on his feet, long hair, and a beard. There was another bright yellow light shining over God's head, and wherever he went, this light moved with him.

"Then God spoke to me. He had a nice, soft, kind voice. As he spoke, I could feel his words inside of me, and this made me feel happy all over. Then the happiness went away and a nice quiet feeling took its place. It spread all through me . . . and it was such a wonderful, peaceful feeling!

"God asked me how I was, if I said my prayers at night, and how I liked my new room. I could hear and see all this going on inside of me. It was so wonderful! Then God left and went back up into the sky on the same path of light he came down on. But what puzzled me was this: how did God know I had a new room?"

The next day Marian talked about the peaceful feelings that went through her body. "When I was coming back to school today after lunch," she said, "I looked up in the sky and suddenly I saw a whole village appear. Then, as I looked again, it disappeared, and a flash of light came down toward me! Right after that I felt a happiness and peacefulness that were not there before. While I was feeling so happy, I got little prickles on my arm as if something was sticking me, and this hurt a little. And then I could see what was doing this. There were little men jabbing me!

"A little later God spoke to me, and I asked him what the pain in my arm was for. He said, 'You have so much happiness in you that you cannot stand it for long, so the pain is to take your mind off the joy for awhile. You can come back to it at another time.'"

Comments Made at a Later Time

Who were these little people mentioned by Marian, and many other children in the past? Were they real, unreal, the imagination, or what?

These little people do exist. They have definite personalities, and they may affect us even though we don't see them. They can be good people or bad people. The little "imps," as Phineas Quimby called them, were troublemakers. The good people, according to the children, were mostly the angels associated with heaven.

It is possible, as I mentioned previously, for a spiritual being to be converted into spiritual energy and vice versa. The size of the little people would then depend on the amount of spiritual energy from which they are formed.

Little people could be units of the personality of a whole spiritual person. They may appear as only parts of the whole person's personality in order to specifically cause sadness, or happiness, or carry on other activities of the whole person. Alternatively, the little people seen by the children may have been the same ones that have existed for centuries: the elves, brownies, fairies, leprechauns, and so on. They could be the "little people" in flying-saucer encounters.

According to Walter Germain's *The Magic Power of Your Mind*, Robert Louis Stevenson once claimed that some of his famous writings were due to little people or, as he called them, his "brownies." His idea for Dr. Jekyll and Mr. Hyde was inspired by them.

Stevenson describes the little people in his book *Across the Plains*, which was written while he took a train ride across the United States. During the night, while Stevenson was half asleep, the brownies would act out scenes for him, and the next day Stevenson would write down what he had seen. Most of the time he didn't know what he would be writing about next until his brownies acted it out.

"My brownies, God bless them!" Stevenson said. "They

do half of my work for me when I'm asleep, and in all likelihood do the rest for me as well when I am wide awake, and I foolishly suppose that I do it myself."

Different people have had different experiences with these little people. Perhaps you, the reader, may have had your own unique experiences, as well, with these little characters!

MUSIC FROM HEAVEN
May 6

The children brought in flowers that they had found growing outdoors to identify and learn about in science class. One girl brought a large bouquet of garden flowers that were mostly tulips and grape hyacinths. During the science period I asked the class, "What happens when you smell flowers?"

I took the bouquet from my desk and walked up and down the aisle. Each child leaned toward the center of the aisle to smell the flowers as I went by. Then they wrote down and drew pictures of any inner experiences they had. Later they described what had occurred, if anything.

Richard said that when he first smelled the flowers, the smell moved inside his body and circled it twice. Several others said they heard singing inside their bodies after they had smelled the flowers.

Brenda said, "I can still hear singing going on inside my body!" I had her come to the front of the room and try to sing what she was hearing inside her body. She tried it, but nothing came out from her lips for awhile. She seemed to be trying to listen to something. Then she sang three different parts of songs—one in English and the rest in Italian, a language she did not even normally speak!

Other children also reported singing. The sounds came into their bodies primarily through the tops of their heads. One girl said the singing came in through her shoulder, and a boy said sounds came in through the sides of his body.

Cathy stood up and said, "I could hear angels singing up in heaven. Then there was a flash of light high up in the sky. The sounds came down in lights of different colors that moved around my body and went into me. I could hear the singing inside of me and around me. Later the sounds went back up into the sky." (See plate 8.)

THE THIRD EYE
June 10

The children were reading aloud from their books, and it was Susan's turn to read. She read about a mother duck and her three ducklings waddling across a barnyard. Then suddenly she stopped reading.

I looked over to see why she had stopped. Susan's eyes were not on the book, but were watching something move across her desk. Her head kept turning to follow whatever it was.

"What's the matter?" I asked her.

"Nothing," she said. "I was just watching the ducks waddle across my desk."

"What ducks?" I asked, surprised.

"The ducks from the book," the girl said. "When I was reading about the ducks in the book waddling across the barnyard, suddenly the words disappeared . . . and instead I saw the ducks on my book—like in real life! They were waddling across my desk!"

Questioning Susan (who was an 'A' student) further, I asked her whether or not this kind of situation often bothered her when she was reading. She said, "No, it doesn't bother me much—only when I read slowly. Then the pictures come out and I see them on the book. When I read faster, the pictures don't have time to come out, and instead I see them inside my head. Then it doesn't bother me at all."

Some years later, when I had a class of twelve-year-old science students, the idea of seeing pictures while reading came up again. I had asked this class of bright science students, "How is it that most of you are able to remember things so well?"

A lively discussion followed, but a comment by one girl named Lisa took me particularly by surprise. She said, "When I read a book, I can see pictures in my head *at the same time*. It's as if I have a *third eye*!"

Curious about this statement, I asked her, "What are the pictures that you see about?"

"They are at the front of the inside of my head, near my forehead area, and they are involved with whatever story I'm reading at the time," the girl responded. "They look somewhat like dreams, but my eyes are still wide open. It is as if I have a small television set in my head."

Later on, when I questioned the rest of the class about the idea of a third eye, most of them expressed that they could actually see pictures in their heads. But when I asked them where the pictures came from, they didn't know. Several students thought the pictures came from some place near the back of their heads, but weren't sure. The pictures had to originate from someplace, and if they did come from the back of the head, what was back there to cause them?

The ancient mystics of the Far East had a clue to the identity of the third eye. They claimed that it was a gland—the pineal gland—located between the two hemispheres of the brain. This pineal gland (which today's medical scientists know very little about) is said to produce a hormone called melatonin. It may be this hormone that causes a child to "see" things.

The pineal gland reaches its maximum size when a person is about seven or eight years old, at which time it also produces the greatest amount of melatonin. After this age, the gland gradually decreases in size until adolescence. After adolescence, very little of the hormone is produced.

So the pineal gland may be the creator of the internal images one sees. These images are "dreamlike pictures"—inspired when one is reading a book, or staring out a window daydreaming, or perhaps at night when one is asleep, dreaming. It is at night that the most melatonin is produced.

All of these images must originate from someplace—most likely one area of the brain. Medical scientists of today seem to be getting closer to finding out where this "image-maker" is located. Recent research at Harvard Medical School indicates that the "generator" of dreams is located near the pineal gland, but the scientists are still not sure. It is my belief that the pineal gland, with its hormone melatonin, is the maker of dreams and the answer to the riddle of the third eye!

PSYCHIC CHILDREN
AND THE NEAR-DEATH EXPERIENCE

What do psychic children have to do with the near-death experience (NDE)? I generally dislike talking about, or writing about, dying. However, psychic children have told me about experiences that sound almost identical to those experienced by people who have been on the verge of death. And these were healthy, happy kids! What is the connection?

The children had these experiences when they put their heads down on their desks to pray in school, or when they knelt down to pray in church, or when they said their prayers before falling asleep. These children had out-of-body experiences. They floated up to the ceiling and looked back and saw their "other body" below. They passed through the ceiling and out into the night, and went wherever their thoughts were concentrated. If their thoughts and prayers were on God, then their spirit bodies moved upward rapidly until they met a "being of light." At that point they felt great happiness, joy, and peace. Sometimes they even saw God!

People having NDEs also experience these things—except they do not usually see God. The Bible says that the pure of heart shall see God, and children have spiritual hearts that are pure, so they see God. Adults may not have spiritual hearts that are totally pure (although perhaps saints almost do). Those with NDEs come close to seeing God when they see a "being of light" in whose presence they feel joy and peace beyond belief.

For both the healthy, happy children and the people with NDEs, the conditions necessary for the spirit body to leave the physical body have been met. In both cases, a person was moving from consciousness to unconsciousness, and at some point in between (in the so-called "twilight zone") the spiritual body left the physical body behind.

When a person is near the point of falling asleep, a separation of the two bodies takes place. Or when a person is hit over the head or becomes very ill, and is in the process of passing out or becoming unconscious, then the physical body can no longer sustain the spirit body and it starts to move out.

When children say prayers in bed and begin to fall asleep, their spirit bodies can travel to wherever their thoughts are. If their thoughts are going to God, then their spirit bodies go there, too. The spirit bodies of dying people, however, usually go automatically toward the heavens and the "being of light."

It may be a profound truth that people on the verge of dying move toward God whether they are religious or not. This may simply be the way life works when transitions are made between heaven and Earth. That is why religion should not have a monopoly on God. God is there for all people—even those without a so-called "religion."

One main difference between a psychic child and a dying person may be the presence of the astral, or silver, cord. As mentioned earlier, this cord connects the physical and spiritual bodies (head to head) and is very elastic. When the spirit body moves a long distance away from the physical body, as when it moves toward heaven, the cord (or, as I call it, the tube through which spiritual energy flows) becomes very thin. It can hold this thinness indefinitely, so the spirit body can always return to the physical body. This information has been researched by Sylvan Muldoon and described in *The Case for Astral Projection.*

In the case of an injured or very ill person, the physical body may not be able to sustain all of the person's spiritual energies, so this energy eventually passes out through the tube and the person "dies." A few people have actually been able to see the cord attached to the physical body finally let go, which is the so-called "end."

In a near-death experience, however, an improvement may take place within the physical body so that the elastic cord, still in place, pulls the spirit body back into the physical body. The person may then go on living.

In my own research work, the children in my classroom said very little about the "dark tunnel" referred to by those having NDEs. The reason may be in the interpretation of the term *tunnel*.

The terms *astral cord* and *silver cord* were also not mentioned

Figure 21. The Tunnel—A Gateway to Heaven. *Elaine saw a tunnel in the sky just as she was on the verge of falling asleep. Then she saw herself (in her spirit body) float upward toward the tunnel. She entered it and went up to heaven.*

by the children. They didn't know these terms. A more accurate term for what the children described might be *tube*, although they seldom used that word. They used the expression *line*, because that is how the energy looked to them. A few children, though, went into more detail, describing it as a transparent, covered tube made of what looked like clear, flexible plastic. Inside it they could see spiritual fluid moving. A few children said they saw the tube grow longer at its tip as the fluid moved swiftly along.

Several children made drawings relating to the tunnel. One girl, Elaine, said she saw it just as she was falling asleep. Her words, along with those of other children, may imply that sleep is a natural out-of-body experience. A drawing of what the tunnel looked like to Elaine is in figure 21.

Another girl, Beatrice, said that as she was falling asleep she rose into the sky as if she were heading toward heaven. Although she didn't mention a tunnel, she did say that along the way she felt herself "falling and tumbling about" several times. This occurred

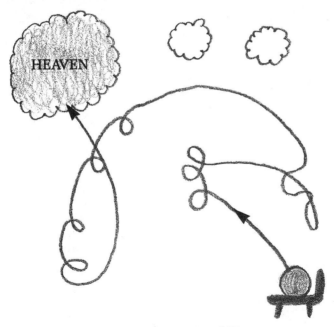

Figure 22. Rising Toward Heaven.

when she started to wake up. But when she continued on to a complete sleep state, she started back upward and then suddenly realized she was in heaven. (A sketch of what she saw is in figure 22.) Beatrice's description of her experience as "falling and tumbling about" is very similar to a description of a man's near-death experience in the book *Life after Life,* by Dr. Raymond Moody.

In all my work with children, NDEs were never brought up. I knew very little about the subject at the time and was not interested in it. I just stressed the positive, good experiences that many children seemed to have. I was never really sure that I was on the right track until I read Dr. Moody's book. His results, to me, were startling and yet inspiring, for they were the best evidence to support the accuracy of my conclusions about my own material.

It is important that the general public believe in both the near-death experience and the children's experiences. They represent some of the best evidence that there is some kind of life after death, that there is somebody up above who is paying attention, and that there is a God. If people don't want to believe this, they can read the Bible, for it describes the very same experiences!

PART IV
Prayers in School

A MOMENT OF SILENT MEDITATION

People get overly excited about the issue of prayers in public school classrooms. To me, this controversy is a lot of nonsense. The situation does not even directly involve emotional adults. It concerns the children in the schools.

When I first started teaching in the public schools, my students were mostly eight-year-olds. At that time, as I mentioned previously, classes could say the Lord's Prayer aloud, but no discussion could take place with the children concerning the prayer.

After teaching third grade for six years, I was moved to the seventh grade to teach science and worked with students who were about twelve years old. By then the prayer requirement in the schools had changed. No prayers were allowed, but the students were required to have a "minute of silent meditation." This is where my troubles began!

Fulfilling the requirement of having the eight-year-old children say their morning prayers was no problem. These kids did it willingly and seemed to have nice looks on their faces afterwards. The twelve-year-old students were a different story, however. I was required to lead them in about a minute of silent meditation. But how do you go about having a class of twelve-year-olds meditate? I wasn't sure how to do this and get positive results.

On the first day of class, I told the students, "We're supposed to have about a minute of silent meditation. To do this, sit quietly for about a minute. As you do so, meditate or think some good thoughts—perhaps to make you feel good and get you started toward having a fine day."

After saying this, I sat down at my desk to have a period of silence for myself. I, also, needed to get some nice thoughts into my mind and start the day off well. So I relaxed in my chair at the front of the class and got ready to put my head down on my desk to meditate, the way I like to do. However, before putting my head down I looked quickly over the classroom to see if the students were going to put their heads down, too. They all just sat there in silence, looking at me.

I thought that, perhaps, after putting my own head down, the students would do the same thing. But after a few days of doing this and then picking up my head, no one else seemed to be putting their head down. Not only that, when I had my head down and couldn't see out over the classroom, some of the students started doing other things. I could hear them whispering to each other, scraping their feet, and so on. This upset me!

Seeing that my approach to the situation was not working, I thought it best to make corrections. So I said, "Starting today, when we have a moment of silent meditation, we will all put our heads down on our desks to meditate."

As they were given a direct order from their teacher, the whole class put their heads down on their desks. I sat down at my desk and put my head down to meditate, as well.

When the minute was almost up, I raised my head to see how the class was doing. Most of them still had their heads down on their desks, but many of them also had turned their heads to the side so they could see their friends in the room. A few were giving facial signals to their friends. This upset me more. I could feel anger boiling up within me! But I had to remain calm and implement the directive of having "a moment of silent meditation" in the classroom so we could start the day off right!

Therefore, the next day I changed my wording around and said, "Today you will put your heads down to meditate, and I don't want to see any of your faces showing!"

The class put their heads down. I, however, instead of sitting down to do the same, thought it better to stand and watch them to be sure they were carrying out my order. Here and there a few faces were still showing, but I stood there glaring at them until they were covered up.

That is how it went for some time. Instead of my starting off the day with nice thoughts, I was probably getting an ulcer. The boys and girls in the class showed no joy on their faces after the period of meditation. A number of them seemed resentful about the whole situation.

There was one boy who, lifting up his head after the meditation period, had sort of a happy look on his face. I wondered why he showed such a positive attitude. So one morning, while he still had that happy look, I headed in his direction. I was curious about what he said in his meditation to produce this happiness.

I asked him quietly, "Why is it that when you lift up your head after meditation you look happy?"

The boy hesitated for awhile. He had a little grin on his face. "I'll tell you," he then said in a low voice, as if not to let others hear him. "At first I was very upset about what we had to do. But then I thought of some words to say that made me feel much better."

"What did you say?" I asked him.

"I kept repeating over and over again one phrase: 'Go to hell! Go to hell! Go to hell!' And this made me happy!"

The boy looked up at me with that little grin on his face, and I looked down at him without saying a word. After all, he had the right to meditate on anything he wished to. I turned away from him and walked away.

After this incident, I gradually forgot about the silent meditation. I was very upset about the whole situation. Twelve-year-old boys and girls were in no mood to meditate. In fact, I felt that the whole attempt was destroying most of the good feelings we had had for each other before we started meditating. This experience with prayer in the classroom was a misery!

However, in my many years of teaching in the public schools, there were only a few such moments of misery to remember. On the whole, my experiences with teaching were good. In particular, my six years with the third grade were perhaps the happiest times of my whole life!

A PROGRAM FOR SCHOOL PRAYERS

How would it be possible to say prayers in the public schools? I would like to offer a suggestion.

First, the word *prayer* should not be used in any way. It brings up too many past biases in people. This word belongs in the same category as "religion," another word it also seems best to avoid. To a child of eight years, words with a similar meaning to that of "prayer" could be "wish" or "hope." When one says, "I hope this can happen" or "I wish that could happen," it comes quite close to prayer.

I would therefore recommend a "period of silent meditation" for schoolchildren *only through the third grade.* Up through that age, nice things can happen to children when they put their heads down on their desks to meditate. Beyond the third grade, however, this process starts losing its value, and by the eighth grade there can be actual resentment of it—and a lot of damage to the children's attitude toward any prayer or meditation.

An experimental program could be set up for one year in the third grade. The "silent meditation" period could be used as an opening exercise to start the day. The teacher could tell the children, when they had their heads down, to think good thoughts and have nice feelings inside. This might help to start everyone off to a good day.

In doing this, ordinary classroom children could quickly become "psychic children," seeing and experiencing things in the spiritual world that adults rarely see or experience. They might therefore be able to reveal much to the adult world about God and God's world. It is in this regard only that the psychic child may be superior to the adult when it comes to knowing God and God's way of life.

The teacher could also tell the children, "When you put your heads down on your desks to meditate, watch and see if anything happens. If something does, try to remember it for later on in the day or week, when you will have a chance to talk about your experience."

Perhaps, as I did with my class, one class period a week could be set aside for the children to talk about their experiences and to do drawings of what they have seen. The teacher could gather such information at the end of the period and then summarize the experiences near the end of the school year.

This program could be carried out for one year to find out if there is any validity to my claims. If there are no positive results with it, the program could be discarded. However, if teachers do experience positive results, as I did, then it could be expanded further, and the results could be published for all to see. This could be the start of one of the most dramatic systems of discovery about life that people on Earth have ever attempted.

KEEPING RELIGION OUT OF THE CLASSROOM

Religion should be kept out of the classroom. If we were to have religion in the schools, whose would it be? Most likely, since the majority of people in the United States are Christian, this is what would be chosen. So where would this leave people of other religions?

Religion has done a lot of good for people of the world, but it has also done a lot of harm. Religious differences separate people from each other. Every group tends to say, "I have the best religion! Join my religion and be saved!" However, there is a way of life that is above religion: having direct contact with God. Such direct spiritual contact could also be called "psychic experience." Almost every major religion has been formed on the basis of one individual's great psychic experience.

I found that many eight-year-old children have had psychic experiences. They could be in direct contact with God and God's world. But a child is in no position to start a new religion from such an experience. Instead, when children talk about such things, parents think it is just their imaginations. Upon hearing her story, one girl's parents said, "Shut up! And don't talk like that anymore!"

God and God's world should not belong only to the churches and synagogues—religions should not have a monopoly on God.

Many people who do not belong to a church or synagogue have more to say about the "living" God than people involved with so-called "religions," and yet such people have no place to express their beliefs. The word *God* should belong to all people. It is their right, just for living on the Earth.

FREE THE CHILDREN!

Children's thoughts about God have been suppressed for centuries, and they are still being suppressed today. This is due to the control the adult world has over children, which adults usually are not even aware of. They put God's way of life under the heading of "religion." However, children talk about God not in a religious sense but as part of a natural way of life.

The Bible, which I would call a historical textbook, speaks in different places about children's relationship to God. In referring to being "born again," it says that if we are not converted and become as children again, we shall not enter the kingdom of heaven. The adult world generally is not aware that ordinary children can become psychic children who see and talk with God. Perhaps children do this the same way the prophets of the Bible did. Children have told me about their experiences with entering heaven. If adults do not want to believe these experiences, they had better throw their Bibles away.

The fact that we do not recognize these abilities in children may be due mainly to the "experts." Child psychologists, who are supposed to study the ways of children and then describe their true nature to parents and others, have not really been able to do so, perhaps because they themselves do not fully understand them. Even the great child psychologist Jean Piaget did not truly understand children. He collected material that was very similar to some of my material, but he did not really understand its nature. Dr. Maria Montessori's comment that the experiences of children may be entirely different from those of adults is worth repeating.

One day a girl from my class met me on the street as she was walking with her mother. The girl started to tell me of a new inner experience she had had the night before. When the mother heard this, she grabbed her daughter by the arm and roughly led her off down the street. I heard her say, "Why do you talk like that! Do you want your teacher to think you're crazy?" The world should not be like this.

Children must be freed from this kind of ignorance. They must be shown understanding and respect for their thoughts and experiences, not shrugged off as "just being imaginative." Their experiences may contain a profound wisdom that could lead the adult world to a better understanding of life or a happier way of life than most of us are now able to realize. And it could be the schools of this country that pave the way for this acceptance and understanding, by initiating a period of silent meditation and discussion in the classroom.

PART V
The Author's Experiences

THOUGHTS ON MY BACKGROUND

Besides being a teacher of science in a public school system for many years, I have also been interested in the religious and psychic worlds. I realize now that my procedure with the children may have been based upon two religious-type experiences that I had before I became a classroom teacher.

The first experience took place about ten years before I began teaching. I was just out of college and in the army, and was standing inside an empty chapel. The second experience occurred about five years after that, when I had finished my wartime duties in Italy and was home on the family farm. I had gone into the mountains to try to make contact with the forces from above because of something that was troubling me. I have included all the details that I can remember about these experiences in the next two chapters.

THE EXPERIENCE IN THE CHAPEL

Toward the beginning of World War II, and after I had finished college, I was inducted into the army and sent off for training at an officers' candidate school. It wasn't long before I was ready and waiting for orders to be shipped overseas to do battle as a lieutenant in the infantry. At that point I was struck by the whole idea of war, and a conflict started to grow within me.

One day at about dusk, as I was walking back to my barracks from the officers' club, the conflict that had been bothering me for several days seemed worse than ever. I had been trained to kill people, and yet I was a kindhearted person who did not want to kill anything or anybody. I didn't know how to resolve this conflict, and it bothered me very much.

I passed an army chapel that was located on the side of the road, and a thought came to me: perhaps God would help me out! I didn't know much about God, but I didn't know where else to turn. This was a Christian chapel, and I was a Jewish fellow, so I felt I probably didn't have much of a chance. But, I thought, I would try anyway. Looking around to make sure no one else was looking, I went back to the chapel, opened the door carefully, and quietly sneaked in, ready to leave if someone else was there.

Once inside, I stood in the back and looked around. There was a single candle burning on the altar, barely lighting up the room. After my eyes became adjusted to the semidarkness, I could see that I was alone except for the figure of Jesus, hanging there on the cross. My eyes went quickly back to the candle, and a little hope flickered within me—perhaps it was meant for me.

"So what do I do now?" I thought to myself. "I should pray to God up above." But I didn't know how to pray, didn't know what to say, and didn't know what to do.

I did a deep-breathing exercise I knew from years back, and this helped drain some of my tension. Then I lifted my head upward and said a few words. I must have done something right, for soon after that things started to change.

I will never forget what happened that day for the rest of my life upon this Earth! It was so awesome, so astonishing, and so beautiful that it will be etched upon my mind forever!

As I stood there alone at the back of the chapel, I suddenly became aware, as if at another level of consciousness, of something taking place high up in the sky. Whatever it was, it was coming down and heading in my direction. It seemed to be a force of some kind. I sensed it coming closer and closer, and then it entered the chapel up by the dome, where it started whirling around and around. It was acting like a wind of some kind.

About the same time I started smelling a sweet aroma, as if some unknown presence had entered the chapel as well. But my attention returned to the whirling force and what it was doing. It came down from above and started wrapping itself around my body—like some living thing. It squeezed me tighter and tighter! It acted like an intelligent force, for it seemed to know what it was doing.

The pressure upon my body became so great that I thought it would crush me, but just as I was about to yell out to God—or whomever it was—to stop, it stopped! The next thing I knew, the force had come into me through the top of my head. I felt it flowing downward to all the parts of my body, even my toes. Then it stopped.

Right after that a feeling of great joy flooded through me. I never knew that such joy could exist upon this Earth—it felt as if it were a "heavenly joy"! Then another feeling swept through me, one of great peace. Such a peacefulness was hard to imagine, unless it were, again, from up above—a "heavenly peace."

As quickly as these two feelings came, they left, and I seemed to be back to my normal self again. However, the force that had entered my body had not left yet. I walked out of the chapel, headed back to my barracks, and went to bed for the night, not realizing that God wasn't through with me yet.

The next day, after having my noonday meal, I was resting on my cot when I suddenly heard the words, "Cleanse thy body!" They came from someplace, but I didn't know where.

Words such as these were not in agreement with my type of thinking. However, I followed the order. The only method that came to me for "cleansing" my body was to take a shower in the nearby shower room. This I did.

When I was finished I dried myself and dressed, but as I started to walk out of the shower room, I suddenly felt very odd! Something peculiar was going on in an area below my stomach. I could feel vibrations starting from that point and spreading out to all the other parts of my body. They were so powerful that they were causing the internal organs in that area to shake. The vibrations filled my whole body and then seemed to want to get out but couldn't.

As I took several steps toward the door to go outside, I felt that

I was not touching the floor—I felt weightless! When I looked down, my feet appeared to be on the floor, but it seemed at that moment that if I had taken a slight jump upward, I would have been able to float into the air!

Then something else happened. The vibrations within me finally got out, and when this happened the feeling of weightlessness disappeared. Then, right before my eyes, light rays started coming out from my body. About twenty such rays spread out in front of me for about fifteen feet.

The light rays were orange-yellow in color, were all on a horizontal plane, and were extending from a point somewhere in my chest. They were rigid and unmoving—somewhat like neon tubes filled with light. Each ray was in the form of a vibrational wave, with each wave being about a foot in length. Whatever direction my chest moved, the rays moved with it.

I seemed under the control of some other intelligent force— most likely the living force that had come down from the sky the night before and entered my body. Also, the great feeling of peace and joy had returned.

As I left the shower room and walked down the boardwalk of the camp, I approached a soldier who was bent over his barracks bag as if he were looking for something inside. When he saw me coming he straightened up and opened his mouth to say something, but no words came out. He just stood there, as if stunned, with his mouth still open.

As I got quite close to him, one of the light rays that was coming from my chest passed right through his body, and I could see it sticking out behind his back. The soldier just stood there, as if transfixed, a look of peace and joy coming over his face as the ray hit him. He was probably feeling the same things that I was.

Finally, the soldier was able to speak, and he asked for the location of a certain place in the camp. I answered him, but I was surprised by the voice that came out of my mouth—it was not my voice, but someone else's. It sounded like a voice of great authority, yet great humility!

Then a wave of great compassion came over me—a compassion for this person standing there. I had never known such a feeling of compassion existed. It was a feeling of a great love for this person, which then seemed to change to a great love for all people on Earth. It was like a "heavenly love" that might come from above and be extended to the entire planet.

Could it be that I had become transhumanized for that moment: a person with heavenly qualities, a feeling of heavenly joy and peace within me, rays of light radiating out from my body, and a voice that showed great authority and yet was filled with deep humility? I didn't know!

This experience didn't last for long — perhaps only a few more minutes. The soldier, after we had spoken, lifted up his barracks bag, swung it over his shoulder, and left. As he did so, the look of peace was still upon his face, but it was combined with a look of bewilderment, as if he didn't know what had happened to him.

A little while later, these extraordinary things stopped happening to me, and I returned to a normal existence. The conflict that had been troubling me before I entered the chapel existed no longer. And if I had previously questioned there being a God someplace up above, never again would I have such doubts!

It wasn't long before I was sent overseas to combat duty in Italy. I carried out all the orders that were given to me for almost six hundred days in a combat area, from Salerno to the Po Valley, without being injured and, to the best of my knowledge, without having to injure anyone else along the way.

THE EXPERIENCE IN THE MOUNTAINS

About five years after the chapel experience, I had my second and only other encounter with the powers of God. It was after the war, and I was back home on the small Connecticut farm where I had grown up. I was about thirty years old and thought it time to get married and settle down.

There were two women I was considering marrying at the time, and I didn't know which one to choose. This bothered me very much. There was Ruby, who was a poet and lived only a few miles away from our farm. I had met her only a few weeks before. And then there was Louisa, a refugee from Italy, whom I was willing to bring to America and marry. After pondering the problem for awhile and being unable to make a decision, I decided to let God give me the answer.

My own parents had struggled and suffered in the past, and I didn't want the same thing to happen to me. There had also been much suffering in the war that I wanted to forget, if possible. If God would give me an answer to my dilemma, perhaps my marriage would be a good one and we would have a good life.

So, on a warm day in early September, I made plans to go off into the mountains that were located on part of our farm. There I would try to contact God. At this stage of my life I felt that I could make this contact with God—I had done it once before in the chapel.

The farm I was raised on had about fifty acres of land, consisting of woods, fields, several streams, a pond, and the beginning of some mountains. They weren't big mountains, but they contained an area where I wanted to go. It was a place that had the key characteristics I needed in order to make my contact with God: solitude and a spot where I could meditate and achieve harmony within my body. These would help shift me to another level of consciousness so that I could become attuned to the spiritual world and, perhaps, God.

First, I needed some things to take up into the mountains with me. Most of the time when I roamed about the woods, I would wear a pair of old shorts cut from a pair of worn trousers. So I chose to wear these comfortable shorts that day. They had plenty of deep pockets, which I filled with the things I needed to contact God: my pipe, tobacco, matches, a stick of gum, and a book.

I left the farmhouse and headed up the dirt road toward the mountains, which were about half a mile away. As soon as I started out, our farm dog spotted me and fell in behind. He was a large animal who looked more like a wolf than a dog.

On this particular day, however, I didn't want the dog with me. I needed solitude and quiet, and the dog usually ran about in the woods chasing squirrels, barking, and rustling old leaves. However, the dog didn't want to go home. So, instead of yelling too much at him and losing the mood I was in, which seemed important to maintain for what lay ahead, I let him come along.

After going up the dirt road a short distance, I cut through the fields, past the apple trees, down to the pond, and then around it along a trail that led through the woods. Then I went up into the mountains a short distance to where a large, flat, rocky ledge jutted out, overlooking the pond.

I knew this area well. As a boy, I had roamed there often and knew where to hear the partridge, where a mother skunk raised her litter of baby skunks, and where there was a trail for the red fox. I knew where the fringed gentian grew in one spot alongside the brook, where the pink lady's slippers could be found underneath the pines, and where the trailing arbutus lay hidden beneath the leaves among the white birches.

These memories came back to me as I followed the trail, especially my fondness for the arbutus, which I used to look for in early spring as it lay hidden beneath the leaves. I would move the leaves away, and there would be the blossoms of this plant. Then I would kneel down and inhale deeply of this fragrant flower. To me it was one of the finest of all aromas in the woods.

I moved on, climbing up the rocky slope to the ledge. Finding a smooth, level spot, I sat down and started taking certain necessary steps, which were the results of an accumulation of past events that made me feel I could make this contact. The answer I wanted from God, in some manner, was which of the two women to marry. I asked this of God because, to me, marriage was a very sacred matter.

From my pockets I took the pipe, tobacco, matches, stick of gum, and book and laid them out in a row next to me. I took off my shoes and my light summer shirt as well—the fewer the restrictions on my body, the greater were the chances of making the contact.

I knew that the key experiences to watch for within myself related to different types of equilibrium. If this was created, then any feelings inside me would disappear, and a sense of "nothingness" would be reached. It was in this state that spiritual experiences usually started to occur.

First I would use the pipe and tobacco to smoke. I wasn't much of a smoker, perhaps smoking only once a day and then only if the mood suited me. However, now it would be an aid to deep breathing, making my exhaled breath visible to me as the smoke flowed outward and away. At the same time, it would help loosen and relax the inner parts of my body. Also, when the tobacco neared the end of its supply within the pipe, the taste would become bitter to my tongue, an important element in my plan.

After smoking, I would put the chewing gum to use, to neutralize the bitter taste. At first the gum would taste quite sweet, but soon this sweetness would lessen and the bitter taste from the pipe tobacco would start fading away. I would be aware of my body's sensations shifting to a balanced point between these two opposite tastes or forces. When that point was reached, I would feel nothing inside. This would be one of the types of equilibrium for which I was looking.

The purpose of the book was to put my thoughts into a mood for meditation. After reading several paragraphs from the right book, I would forget the book and allow my own thoughts to take over. These thoughts would soon be soaring in grand style, trying to figure out the mysteries of the world.

At different times of my life, various books have seemed to fit this mood best. When I was a soldier in the war, I carried a copy of *The Robe* by Lloyd Douglas in my hip pocket and read it whenever there was time. After the war, Emerson's essays fitted the mood. Then books by Tagore worked for awhile. My current choice was a small black book, *The Prophet*, written by the Lebanese poet Kahlil Gibran.

After seating myself on the most level area near the center of the rocky ledge, with my legs folded in front, I proceeded to fill my pipe with tobacco. (Most of the commercial tobaccos were too strong for me, and I always searched for the mildest tobacco I could find.) After lighting the pipe, I looked about.

The dog could be heard someplace off in the woods, racing about and rustling leaves. Sitting there quietly, I could feel some of the pressures inside my body draining away and parts of my body going limp.

Picking up the book, I read awhile. I don't remember which section it was, but it was enough to stimulate my mind and start me meditating on my own. What I meditated on, I also don't remember.

However, I do remember the dog. He was starting to make me mad! He was chasing a squirrel, and I could see them both. The dog's barking filled the woods, spoiling the silence I needed to maintain the correct frame of mind. Then, luckily, the squirrel led the dog out of sight, and they did not bother me anymore that day.

The burning pipe was reaching the end of its tobacco, and the taste on my tongue was becoming bitter. Setting the pipe aside, I took the chewing gum, put it into my mouth, and chewed it slowly. The sweet taste soon started to diminish the bitter taste.

The point of equilibrium I was watching for was halfway between these two tastes, where both the bitter taste from the tobacco and the sweet taste of the gum would be gone. Then there would be a feeling of "nothingness." I could feel this point approaching. Finally, when I reached it, I moved the gum to the back of my mouth and out of the way.

I stretched out fully on the cool rock. The coldness was soothing against my warm, bare back. Even though it was early September, it was a very warm day. My body was warm, but the woods and rock were cool. This balance of the hot and cold created another point of equilibrium that would help me make contact with the forces from above.

I started concentrating my thoughts on achieving this equilibrium within myself. I could feel the coldness of the rock moving up into my body, and I could feel the warmness moving down and out. Then a balance was reached between the heat and the cold within me. I moved my thoughts away, to leave that point of equilibrium in place.

Stretched out on the rocky ledge, I shifted my thinking to my breathing so I could further relax any parts of my body that might be tense. This was crucial if I were to make contact with God.

The key point in the breathing process was at the end of exhalation. At this point, when the air in the lungs was exhaled, I waited perhaps four or five seconds before starting to take in air again. It was at that point in time that the contact could also be made. This was another point of equilibrium, and it might be the secret to contacting God, if this were to happen at all.

Slowly, I filled my lungs with as much air as they could hold. I held it in for awhile, then slowly let it drain out. Then I waited four or five seconds before filling my lungs again. I kept repeating this process, and I could feel my body getting limper and limper. It was feeling especially heavy on the hard rock under me.

Finally, I felt there was nothing else I could do. Now I had to wait for something to happen. How long this would take or what it would be, I did not know. At no time did I directly ask God for help, but I assumed that he knew my problem and would respond without needing any formal declaration.

The inner condition of my body seemed to be attuned and receptive to the spiritual world I was trying to contact. My breathing shifted to shallow breaths so as not to alter my inner feeling from the point of adjustment I had reached. It seemed as if my body was in a state of suspended animation and that I was at another level of consciousness.

By now, perhaps fifteen minutes had passed since I had first come to the rock. Suddenly, high up above me in the treetops, I noticed a movement of some kind. Something was fluttering straight toward me. Was this a sign from God?

Then I saw what it was—a lacewing, a flying insect with delicate, pale green wings and a fairylike appearance. The lacewing fluttered straight toward me and stopped about two feet above my body. It hovered there for awhile. Then it moved slowly straight back up into the air to the treetops from where it came. I wondered if this was some sort of sign, but I didn't think so.

There was nothing else to do but wait a little longer. I continued to lie there, although my body was starting to ache a little as I lay on the hard rock. Suddenly I heard something! There was a sound happening some distance away — beyond the trees. It was a roaring kind of noise. And then I recognized it: it was the sound of a powerful wind! The roaring sound got louder and louder as it came closer and closer.

I turned my head to see what was going on. Off to my right, about two hundred feet away, the treetops started swaying violently. The wind was sweeping through them and heading in my direction!

I watched the wind as it approached. Its path seemed to be about twenty-five feet across, based on the number of trees that were swaying, and it was located up near the tops of the young trees, which were about thirty feet tall.

The wind roared closer and then, when it was just above me in the treetops, it stopped! The woods become suddenly still again. Only five or six seconds had elapsed from the time I had first sighted the wind.

What was this wind? It was the power of God! I knew this from my experience in the chapel.

So God had responded. What next? I waited for a further response, but nothing was happening. It seemed like I waited a long time, lying there on the rock, trying to keep that feeling of emptiness inside my body. Perhaps the wind was the only sign I would be getting from God, and there would be no answer to my problem.

Finally, I decided to wait just one more minute before heading for home without an answer. In that one minute I would try my best to achieve a finer attunement within myself by resuming the breathing practice.

After several more breaths, I became still. I lay there limp, not moving a muscle. Suddenly a hush seemed to come over the woods—a peculiar type of a hush. And then I heard a voice— loud and clear! It was a voice that had a deep, resonant tone, a voice of great authority. It spoke one word: "Ruby!"

The voice sounded as if it came from somebody in front of me, but I could see no one. It seemed to come from about eight or ten feet away.

Who spoke to me that I was unable to see? Perhaps, I thought, it was a messenger from God. Whoever it was, it spoke the one word that gave me an answer to my problem.

I had gone off into the mountains to seek God's advice and had attuned my body to be receptive to God's power. A wind came, stopping above me, and I knew from past experience that

God's power moves like a wind. I clearly heard a voice that gave an answer.

So what further proof did I need? Was I to have doubts about whether or not it was God who sent the answer? I was satisfied enough that it was so. The only thing that would have been better, perhaps, would have been if my body had been more finely attuned so that I could have seen the spiritual person who stood in front of me to speak the word "Ruby."

What else was there to do? I had my answer. Before getting up from the rock, though, I did one more thing. I brought the chewing gum that had been tucked away at the back of my mouth forward again. I would use it to sort of "seal the marriage" here on the rock.

Taking the gum from my mouth, I formed it into the shape of a heart. Reaching up to an overhanging piece of rock above me, I pressed the "heart" deep into the rocky surface. Then, feeling that it was time to go, I loaded my pockets with the things I had brought and headed for home.

Several months later, Ruby and I were married. A few months after that, a doctor told her she had a serious kidney condition and probably had only a few more years to live. But Ruby lived on, and we had a happy marriage for twenty-eight years before she passed away. To me, this marriage was the closest thing I have experienced to "heaven on Earth."

In her life, Ruby knew God perhaps better than I did. Her poetry, published throughout the United States and in foreign countries as well, often talked about God and heaven above. One of her last poems, which reflects some of her thinking, follows:

One Appointment

Consider, visitor, this one appointment
And use time well
For there will be no second invitation
To ring the bell.

Be happy, laugh, distribute joy to others
For they, like you
Are guests for their brief day before they too
Are elsewhere due.

Bring nothing more than spirit for this stay,
Come as you are,
And covet nothing, for yourself will seek
Another star.

CONCLUSION

The material in these pages is only one man's version of what took place—mine. I have tried to be as accurate and as honest as I possibly could.

The original names of the children have been changed so to respect their privacy. These children are now grown up, for a long time has gone by, and most of them probably are now married, have families, and are leading normal lives. If they were questioned now about what I wrote in this book, I feel that they would probably not remember what they said then. When they were eight years old, things happened so fast for them within the spiritual world that their experiences would have been, most likely, quickly forgotten.

The conversations with the children in this book are quite close to the words actually used. They were taken from my many notes, which were recorded while the words were still fresh in my mind.

The original drawings by the children were made with colored crayons. The figures in this book are close copies of the originals, done both in black and white and in color.

The most significant proof of these children's experiences that I still have, after all these years, is the notebooks and several thousand drawings that are up in my attic. All of these were made at the time the research was under way. Out of all the drawings, I chose only the most simple ones, those I could understand, to be included in this book.

I have explained the method I used to conduct my research in this book. Any other teacher, researcher, or scientist, with the proper type of understanding, could follow the same method and verify what has been written here. I strongly believe that if my information about the lives of children turns out to be true, it could be one of the great discoveries of our time.

Here ends my story. I've told it as best I could. I'm getting along in years now, and before it's my turn to move on, I wanted to tell others about the children's experiences with God, about my experiences with God, and about the woman, Ruby, the wife who was chosen for me by God!

BIBLIOGRAPHY

Armstrong, Thomas. *The Radiant Child*. Wheaton, IL: Quest Books, 1985.

Asch, Sholem. *Moses*. New York: Pocket Books.

Bristol, Claude M. *The Magic of Believing*. Englewood Cliffs, NJ: Prentice-Hall, 1948.

Bucke, Richard M., M.D. *Cosmic Consciousness*. New York: University Books, 1961.

Burrows, Millar. *The Dead Sea Scrolls*. New York: The Viking Press, 1955.

Coles, Robert. *The Spiritual Life of Children*. Boston: Houghton Mifflin, 1990.

David-Neel, Alexandra. *Initiations and Initiates in Tibet*. New York: University Books, 1959.

_____. *Magic and Mystery in Tibet*. New York: University Books, 1958.

Dresser, Horatio W. *Health and the Inner Life*. New York: G.P. Putnam's Sons, 1906.

Ferguson, Marilyn. *The Aquarian Conspiracy*. Boston: J.P. Tarcher, 1980.

Fox, Oliver. *Astral Projection*. New York: University Books, 1962.

Frazer, James. *The Golden Bough*. New York: Macmillan, 1945.

Gibran, Kahlil. *The Prophet*. New York: Alfred A. Knopf, 1945.

Germain, Walter M. *The Magic Power of Your Mind*. New York: Hawthorn Books Inc., 1956.

Govinda, Lama Anagarika. *Foundations of Tibetan Mysticism*. New York: E.P. Dutton, 1960.

James, William. *Varieties of Religious Experiences*. New York: Modern Library, 1929.

Johnson, Raynor C. *The Imprisoned Splendour*. New York: Harper & Row, 1953.

King James Version of *The Holy Bible*. New York: Grosset & Dunlap, 1959.

Kübler-Ross, Elisabeth. *On Children and Death*. New York: Macmillan, 1985.

_____. *On Death and Dying.* New York: Macmillan, 1970.

Maslow, Abraham H. *Religions, Values, and Peak Experiences.* New York: Viking Press, 1970.

Masters and Houston. *The Varieties of Psychedelic Experience.* New York: Dell Publishing Co., 1966.

Mitchell, Janet L. *Out-of-Body Experiences.* New York: Ballantine Books, 1981.

Montessori, Maria. *The Secret of Childhood.* New York: F.A. Stokes Company, 1939.

Moody, Raymond A., Jr., M.D. *Life after Life.* New York: Mockingbird Books/Bantam, 1976.

Muldoon, Sylvan. *The Case for Astral Projection.* Chicago: The Aries Press, 1936.

Myers, F.W.H. *Human Personality and its Survival of Bodily Death.* New York: University Books, 1961.

Peterson, James W. *The Secret Life of Kids.* Wheaton, IL: Quest Books, 1987.

Purce, Jill. *The Mystic Spiral.* New York: Avon Books, 1974.

Reich, Wilhelm. *Cosmic Superimposition.* Rangeley, ME: Orgone Institute Press, 1951.

Sherman, Harold. *How to Know What to Believe.* Greenwich, CT: Fawcett Publications, 1976.

Standing, E.M. *Maria Montessori, Her Life and Work.* New York: New American Library, 1962.

Stevenson, Robert Louis. *Across the Plains.* Cambridge, MA: Belknap Press of Harvard University Press, 1966.

Sudre, René. *Parapsychology.* New York: Citadel Press, 1960.

Swedenborg, Emanuel. *Arcana Coelestia* (Heavenly Secrets). 12 vol. New York: Swedenborg Foundation, 1974.

_____. *Divine Love and Wisdom.* Translated by George Dole. New York: Swedenborg Foundation, 1986.

_____. *Heaven & Hell.* New York: Swedenborg Foundation, 1984.

_____. *Spiritual Life—The Word of God.* New York: Swedenborg Foundation, 1971.

Underhill, Evelyn. *Mysticism.* New York: Meridan Books, 1955.

_____. *Worship.* New York: Harper & Row, 1936.

Waite, Arthur. *The Holy Kabbalah.* New York: University Books, 1960.

Williams, Michael, ed. *They Walked with God.* Greenwich, CT: Fawcett
  Publications, Inc., 1957.

Wilson, Colin. *Afterlife.* New York: Doubleday & Co., 1987.

ABOUT THE AUTHOR

Samuel Silverstein grew up in the country in the New England area. He went to college with the intention of becoming a scientist, but after graduating he was drafted into the U.S. armed services during World War II and became an officer (lieutenant) with a combat infantry unit in Italy. Not wanting to carry the gun that was issued to him, he was able to "exchange" it for a pair of binoculars . . . and went through the entire Italian campaign—almost six hundred days—as a reconnaissance officer near the front lines without being injured or injuring anyone.

After the war, he took additional college courses to become a teacher instead of a scientist. His first assignment was teaching third-grade children in a public school, which he did for six years. It was during this time that he carried on his research with the eight-year-old students as described in this book. For the next twenty-seven years, he taught science to twelve-year-olds at a junior high school, using some of the principles he later discovered had been put forth by the famous educator Maria Montessori. Silverstein retired from his teaching career in 1985, and today spends his days at his home in Connecticut, studying nature and trying to live a peaceful life.

Silverstein married an author and poet, who had six books published before she passed away after twenty-eight years of marriage. Their daughter is a poet and their son, an artist.

BOOKS OF RELATED INTEREST
BY BEAR & COMPANY

BREATHING
Expanding Your Power and Energy
by Michael Sky

EMERGENCE OF THE DIVINE CHILD
Healing the Emotional Body
by Rick Phillips

ILLUMINATIONS OF HILDEGARD OF BINGEN
Text by Hildegard of Bingen
Commentary by Matthew Fox

INNER CHILD CARDS
A Journey into Fairy Tales, Myth & Nature
by Isha Lerner & Mark Lerner

KEEPERS OF THE FIRE
Journey to the Tree of Life Based on Black Elk's Vision
by Eagle Walking Turtle

ORIGINAL BLESSING
A Primer in Creation Spirituality
by Matthew Fox

THE PRAYING FLUTE
Song of the Earth Mother
by Tony Shearer

Contact your local bookseller or write:
BEAR & COMPANY
P.O. Drawer 2860
Santa Fe, NM 87504